A Who's Who
of Australian and
New Zealand Film Actors:
The Sound Era

by

SCOTT PALMER

The Scarecrow Press, Inc.
Metuchen, N.J., & London
1988

Library of Congress Cataloging-in-Publication Data

Palmer, Scott, 1958-
    A who's who of Australian and New Zealand film
actors.

    Bibliography: p.
    1. Motion picture actors and actresses--
Australia--Credits. 2. Motion picture actors and
actresses--New Zealand--Credits. I. Title.
PN1998.2.P35 1988   791.43'028'0922   87-32215
ISBN 0-8108-2090-0

DEDICATED TO

RENEE

CONTENTS

AUTHOR'S NOTE

The following pages list Australian and New Zealand motion picture actors whose main body of work was done in films of the sound era. To list every performer is not possible; I have endeavored to list those whose film careers were either in the United States, Great Britain, or Australia, including a complete list of each performer's film credits.

Years of birth and death are listed for each performer when they could be traced. Since a number of "new" performers are included in this book that cannot be found elsewhere, their dates were unavailable for inclusion. A brief character description is also given, followed by the list of films, in chronological order. I have tried to give the original title of the film and the year it was completed as well. I have also listed television films.

I would like to thank the following performers for their assistance to me in my research of their film careers: Dorothy Alison, Allan Cuthbertson, Trader Faulkner, Sir Robert Helpmann, Leo McKern, Murray Matheson, Clive Revill, and Ewen Solon; my special thanks also go to Pat Perilli of the Library Services Department of the British Film Institute.

Finally, I welcome and appreciate any advice, comments, criticisms or the like, which can be addressed to me at 2645 Teresita Street, San Diego, California 92104.

Scott Palmer
San Diego, 1987

INTRODUCTION

The motion picture industry in Australia at present is at the
highest level of both output and quality than anytime in the
more than ninety years of its history. In the following pages,
the evolution, changes, and development of the industry will
be discussed.

Australia in the latter part of the nineteenth century was
experiencing economic growth and prosperity, which was reflected in the growing number of music halls, vaudeville houses,
and "straight" theaters, which were especially popular in the
cities of Sydney, Melbourne, Perth and Adelaide.

Australia's primary industry at that time was ranching
(sheep and cattle); a serious drought in 1891-92 took its toll
on the industry. This disaster was reflected in economic fail-
ures of virtually every kind throughout the whole of Australia;
naturally theatergoers in Australia at this time were affected
along with everyone else. Even reduced admissions did little
to guarantee success in the theaters.

"Motion pictures" first appeared in London in 1895 with
an untitled Kinetoscope comedy, directed by and starring one
of the pioneers of motion pictures, Birt Acres (1854-1918).
Acres followed the techniques of William Friese-Greene (1855-
1921), who has often been credited with "discovering" motion
pictures.

The "filming" was generally done out of doors, and for a number of years these early motion pictures were only about a hundred feet in length, which translates to about three minutes running time.

The first actual "motion picture" seen in Australia was shown at the Melbourne Opera House on August 22, 1896, and presented by the American-born magician Carl Hertz. Shown on a machine which he had bought from R. W. Paul (another renowned early film pioneer who had developed it in 1894), Hertz had originally intended to use the device to augment his conjuring tricks. However, Hertz was bright enough to realize the impact that the first really worthwhile moving picture camera would have; he toured New Zealand, South Africa, Asia, India, and the Orient with this new invention. On that August Saturday evening in Melbourne, he amazed critics with the 23-minute film. Journalists who covered the event were quick to take note that here was more than a novel gimmick; a new era was about to unfold.

In September of 1896, Walter Barnett, a former photographer, and Marius Sestier, entrepreneur, joined forces and made in Sydney what is probably the first actual motion picture filmed in Australia. It also was the first of a series of short films which ran over fifty feet in length (about $2\frac{1}{2}$ minutes). In November of the same year, Sestier also filmed the prestigious Melbourne Cup. This attracted a wide audience even at the (then) expensive price of two shillings per person.

By 1897 writers were being hired to script "stories," or screenplays, as we would refer to them now. It was at this time that the Salvation Army, Melbourne branch, became actively involved with the production of films in the fledgling motion picture industry in Australia.

Through subscriptions from the public in general, as well as from private citizens who craved anonymity, the Salvation Army began to rapidly produce large numbers of short-length films which were aimed at showing the operations of its organization. The group's overall aims were not nearly so much in the nature of a show business or financial gains venture; rather like Lord J. Arthur Rank several decades later, the Salvation Army was primarily concerned with spreading the religious word, in this case through the medium of film. However, audience enthusiasm proved so great, especially in 1898, that

on many occasions the group was compelled to repeat the program as soon as it was finished to placate the viewers.

By 1899 the Salvation Army was producing a number of
these short films, which were generally five minutes in length.
In 1900, the Army filmed an ambitious production entitled,
Soldiers of the Cross; when it opened in September of 1900
one could easily see the amount of research as to detail that
had gone into it. Its authenticity greatly impressed both the
general audience as well as the journalists and reporters as-
signed to view it.

Up to this time, films in Australia were shown in theaters,
music halls, and vaudeville houses, and usually followed the
main programs, i.e., plays, vaudeville and comedy acts, musical
performances, etc. The reason for this is that films at the
time, and for several years yet, were still very short in length;
most of them did not exceed ten minutes' time. Also, a good
many of them were shown out of doors, even in public streets
where the large spaces could accommodate more people. Most
of the films seen then were newsreels of current events; it
was not until a few years later that "story" films would become
a popular form of entertainment in Australia.

By 1905, arrangements had been made for the distribution
and importation of films from places like England and America,
and there was rapid and widespread growth in the market.
People who had previously never seen motion pictures were
now being able to see them locally rather than having to jour-
ney to the larger cities.

One of the early well-known motion pictures made in
Australia was produced in 1906 by the Tait brothers, who
were early pioneer film producers. It depicted the life and
death of a notorious Australian outlaw, Ned Kelly, who had
developed a sort of cult following not unlike that of Jesse
James in the United States.

This was a landmark film for several reasons. Firstly,
during its viewing, audiences were given a little booklet in
order to make the story somewhat clearer. Secondly, the
actual story was painstakingly researched through newspaper
articles; probably up to this time it was the most authentic
film to be made in Australia. Also, a good deal of it was filmed

on actual locations. The outdoor scenes, much different from
what audiences of the long-running play on the same subject
were used to, did much to create an aura of nationalism and
authenticity.

Audiences recognized the quality of the production,
which ran over an hour in length and was undoubtedly the
longest Australian motion picture produced up to that time.
The film was accompanied by lectures, and also (rather the-
atrically), later on, live sound effects were incorporated at the
showings.

The overwhelming positive response to this particular film
helped to open the door for feature film production in Australia
immediately. Regular production soon commenced for what had
previously been considered lengthy motion pictures; in this
respect the film industry in Australia was taking steps to sur-
pass that of other countries.

Distributors and exhibitors of film in Australia, particularly William Gibson and his associate Millard Johnson, were now
major forces in the burgeoning Australian motion picture industry. Not only were they and others importing and distri-
buting films made in other countries, but they also played a
significant part in the distribution and production of domestic
motion pictures.

One of the main problems that occurred with the exporta-
tion of Australian-made films was their lack of worldwide appeal.
The remedy for this was to come up with a film that could be
universally identifiable, but this was some time off.

Another significant film in early Australia was For the
Term of His Natural Life, taken from a novel which had in
turn been adapted into a stage play. (The film was remade
successfully some 75 years later, also in Australia.) This was
in 1908, and in Australia at that time, and immediately after-
wards, a good many motion pictures were derivatives from
stage plays.

By 1910, motion picture houses were springing up all over
Australia, as exhibitors now began to see the advantages of
leasing theaters or halls for the sole purpose of showing films.
One of the early exponents of theater leases and purchase was
T. J. West, who by 1911 operated some two dozen theaters, the

most famous of which was the Olympia-Melbourne, which had
a seating capacity of 5,000.

The public was now, in the pre-war years, giving great
support to this new form of entertainment, which led to a number of foreign (specifically British, French, and American)
distribution companies and agencies being set up in Australia.

Raymond Longford, a merchant seaman, and Lottie Lyall,
a stage actress, emerged as the most popular Australian motion picture stars at the time, appearing together in a number
of films, most of which were financed by a British corporation.
A good many of their films were shot out of doors rather than
inside studios, which not only created a flavor of authenticity,
but also kept down production costs. It was not uncommon for
a film to make a profit by the end of its first week of release.
Most of the motion pictures in this way were also shot in a week
or ten days.

Fred Niblo, Ronald Conway, John Cosgrove, Shirley Ann
Richards, R. L. "Snowy" Baker, Charles Villiers, Roy Rene,
Gilbert Emery, and Arthur Tauchert were now establishing
themselves as popular stars of the Australian cinema. Raymond
Longford, in addition to acting in films. was also gaining a reputation as a fine director of early Australian pictures. One
of his notable achievements was Australia Calls, which depicted
the aeroplane and starred W. E. Hart.

For Australia, which was made in 1915 and starred the
British actor Boyd Irwin, was another significant early feature,
as was Mutiny on the Bounty, one of many versions of the
famous story, which was made in 1915 and starred George Cross
and Lottie Lyall.

With the outbreak of the First World War, filmmaking came
to a standstill for the most part in Europe. But not in Australia,
where the opposite was occurring; in fact, film production was
at its highest level, one which would not be surpassed for some
sixty years.

Australia had always had a strong reputation for the production of fine documentaries, and it was during this period
that it really developed. One of the early pioneers in this field
was the explorer Francis Birtles, who saw motion pictures as
a way to publicize his numerous expeditions (as well as those

of other explorers), which he felt would be useful in garnering
subscriptions from the public in order to assist the financing
of future expeditions. His very well-received chronicle entitled "Home of the Blizzard" (1913) and later ventures in col-
laboration with filmmaker Frank Hurley, among them the notable
Into Australia's Unknown (1914), not only earned him the reputation as the leading Australian documentarist, but also helped
in the funding of Shackleton's next expedition to the pole. It
was this expedition that Hurley has recorded in what is considered to be his masterpiece, In the Grip of the Polar Ice, which
was released in 1917 and depicted the grueling two-year jour-
ney which by now has become legendary.

Birtles continued to make documentaries, although the lack of
public interest limited his work. Among the better of his
later documentaries were Across Australia in the Track of
Burke and Wills, Through Australian Wilds: Across the Track
of Ross Smith, Australia's Lovely Lands, and Coorab in the
Island of Ghosts.

During the First World War, Australian films got greater
distribution, not only abroad but in Australia itself, as European film production was on the decline, at least temporarily.
At the time, American film production was on the rise; the
United States would not enter the war until 1917. American
distributors soon began to realize that the Australian market
had great value, and in 1914-15 a number of U.S. motion picture
companies set up exchanges or outlets in Australia, including
Metro (later to become M-G-M), Fox, Paramount, and First
National.

Australian films began to draw their subject matter from
the war: Australia at War (1914), It's a Long Long Way to
Tipperary (1914), Hero of the Dardanelles (1915), Anzac
V.C.s (1915), The Day (1916), Murphy of Anzac (1916),
Australia Prepared (1917), and Australia's Peril (1917) were
significant films made in Australia during this time. (Note:
the word "Anzac" refers to a member of the Australian and
New Zealand Army Corps.) These films were made with the ap-
proval of the Australian government and did much to arouse
in young men the patriotic fervor which in turn assisted en-
listments.

Australian nationalistic feelings were running high during

the war, especially at its beginning; this was a theme which certainly caught the attention of filmmakers worldwide as well as the Australian ones. The threat of German spies, a fear which had been heightened of late by the ever-increasing expansion of territories in the Pacific by Germany, was also on everyone's mind.

Filmmakers quickly began to make films about espionage. How We Beat the Emden (1915) depicted the battle (the first to be won by the Australian Navy) between the Australian ship Sydney and the German cruiser Emden. Also in 1915, a somewhat fictionalized account of German spies was told in For Australia, which was followed by the films If the Huns Come to Melbourne in 1916 and Australia's Peril in 1917, both of which showed what might happen if the Germans were to invade Australia. These films and others may have had a direct influence on the government; soon there was a plea for compulsory military conscription.

Not everyone supported the war with patriotic sentiments. In fact, a large section of Australian society opposed the war, which ultimately was responsible for the national strike which involved in excess of 100,000 workers in August-September of 1917. The Great Strike was a film that presented a sympathetic depiction of the workers. Not surprisingly, it was opposed by the government, which finally agreed to release the film under the title, Recent Industrial Happenings in New South Wales, in a toned-down, edited version.

Several months later, the first in what was to be a series of films starring Reginald L. "Snowy" Baker was begun. It was entitled The Enemy Within (1917) and dealt with a group of German subversives and spies who were to have infiltrated all levels of Australian society. These people were shown to be a leading cause of political, social, and economic unrest in Australia.

The J. C. Williamson film company was also prominent in making propagandistic motion pictures, such as Broken Hill on New Year's Day Massacre (1915), Making Wool into Khaki Cloth (1916), Australia at War (1916), and Australasian Gazette (1918), the last concerned with the production, manufacture, and use of artificial limbs that was taking place in Sydney at the Victoria Barracks.

The year 1918 was most prolific for the Australian film industry up to that point, although only eighteen feature films were made, quite a small figure by today's standards.

Beaumont Smith was the consummate combination of film-maker, entrepreneur, and showman. A former businessman and journalist, Smith seemed to know how to concoct just the right combination of national spirit with interesting plots and melodrama; audiences certainly enjoyed his films, which originally were accompanied by a traveling midget circus called "Tiny Town."

Smith's series about the Hayseeds, a rural Australian family, gained wide popularity; features in the series included Our Friends the Hayseeds, The Hayseeds Come to Town, The Hayseeds' Backblocks Show, The Hayseeds' Melbourne Cup, Prehistoric Hayseeds, and Townies and Hayseeds.

Aside from the Hayseed comedies, Smith also filmed a number of melodramas, notably Satan in Sydney (1918), which dealt with the influence of foreigners in Australia (in this case, the Chinese), and Desert Gold (1919), which concerned a racehorse. Although Smith included gimmicky technical things in his films, the productions attracted large audiences. There are certain parallels with these films and the serials that were popular later on in Hollywood during the thirties and forties. Smith's films would be shot in three or four weeks, and he would often take them on tour, enhancing their flavor by shooting additional scenes on location and incorporating them into the films. In that way (another gimmick) they appealed to people on a local basis.

Although Beaumont Smith was criticized by other filmmakers for lack of plot or story originality as well as technical indifferences, the public seemed to take the opposite view. Smith's films were as least financially, if not necessarily critically, successful.

After the war, social, political, and economic conditions and attitudes were changing. Isolationism was dying in the hearts and minds of Australians; a new sense of national pride was replacing it. However, while most embraced this new national pride, many, many others desired even stronger ties with Great Britain.

Raymond Longford, who already had established himself
as an actor and director, was, in the immediate post-war years,
to become one of the most prominent directors in Australian
films. A noteworthy production was his 1918 motion picture
entitled A Sentimental Bloke, which was taken from the ex-
tremely successful poetry/verse book Songs of a Sentimental
Bloke by C. J. Dennis, published three years earlier. The
sequel to this book, written by Dennis the following year (1916)
was called The Moods of Ginger Mick, also later to be filmed on
several occasions.

Longford's film starred the comedian Arthur Tauchert and
the (by this time) quite popular Lottie Lyall, with whom Longford had already appeared as an actor in a number of films just
a few years previously. This film is a perfect example of Longford's intertwining of humanistic values and comedic timing
with a sense of the sentimental. When the film was released, it
broke all previously held box-office and attendance records for
an Australian film. It was not uncommon to find it playing to
standing-room-only crowds throughout the whole of Australia.
Not only was the film a commercial triumph, but critics every-
where were unanimous in their praise.

Longford then made The Adventures of Ginger Mick in 1920,
which was also well received. The film adroitly combined humor
and pathos, which culminated in the final scene when Mick is
heroically killed at the battle of Gallipoli.

Later that same year, Longford directed a film entitled
On Our Selection, which held to the conviction of rural
Australia as the future rather than urbanization, which was actually inevitable. Once again Longford based his film on a book
that had been written by Steele Rudd and later turned into a
highly successful stage play. This motion picture also had the
characters that Rudd had created (he also called them the Rudd
family) and presented a rather warmhearted, humanistic but at
the same time authentic picture of the common folk. The film was
critically praised both for its realistic flavor and for its lack of being overly sentimental.

The following year, 1921, Longford presented a sequel
entitled Rudd's New Selection, which was more of a satirical
pastiche on the highly popular characters of Australia's best
loved bush family, the Rudds. It starred J. P. O'Neill and Tal

Ordell as Dad and Dave Rudd, respectively; once again Lottie
Lyall appeared as Nell.

Longford's following film, also made in 1921, was quite a
different type than he had previously tackled. Up to now,
Longford had mainly directed films with lighthearted content,
but with The Blue Mountain Mystery, he dealt with quite a
different subject. The film was based on the murder mystery
The Mount Marunga Mystery by Harrison Owen, and Longford
turned it into quite an excellent film.

Another respected contemporary of Longford in this same
period was the director Franklyn Barrett, who, like Longford,
was acutely aware of the nationalistic sentiments that were
prevalent in Australia at the time; this is reflected in his films.
Barrett, who had been directing films in Australia before the
war, was now using realistic techniques and approaches in
his motion pictures, initiating a quasidocumentary style.

One of Barrett's more important features was called The
Breaking of the Drought, which was taken from a stage play
which in turn had been based on the actual catastrophic true-
life drought of the late nineteenth century. This film showed
the struggles of the rural people, who were hit hardest by the
drought, and showed them as fierce strugglers who grittily
overcame adversity.

Barrett himself favored the country folk over city dwellers,
and this attitude was reflected in his next film, The Girl of
the Bush, which was made in 1921. He portrayed the big city
itself as almost a den of iniquity, where corruption and loose
morals ran rampant. This film was better received by the public,
and critics also made praiseworthy comments.

Following the success of The Girl of the Bush, Barrett
also in 1921 embarked on a venture that was to be called Know
Thy Child, concerning the delicate themes of incest and il-
legitimacy, subjects that were quite unusual for a film of that
period in Austrialia.

In spite of a wide publicity compaign and superior technical
quality (not to mention the unusual theme of the film), Know
Thy Child was a financial failure. As a result, Barrett made
only one more motion picture, The Rough Passage (released in
1922) before he retired from films.

One of the reasons for the failure of Know Thy Child,
and indeed for a financial predicament concerning a good many
Australian films at that time, was, in part, the unsatisfactory
new contract system that distributors and exhibitors of films
in Australia were being forced to use. Also, the widespread
importation of foreign films, particularly American (Hollywood
at this time in the early twenties was supplying well in excess
of half the world market of films, and nine out of every ten
films showing in Australia were those imported from the United
States), was deflating the Australian production market.

In the early part of the twenties, numerous films were
made in Australia by a variety of different directors who were
trying in vain to compete with the influx of Hollywood films.
Among notable productions at the time were The Man from
Kangaroo (1920), The Shadow of Lightning Ridge (1920), The
Jackaroo of Coolabong (1920), all vehicles starring Snowy
Baker; Silks and Saddles (1921), The True Story of the Ned
Kelly Gang (1921), Sunshine Sally (1922), The Throwback
(1922), Circumstance (1922), and The Dinkum Bloke (1923).

During the 1920s, the Australian Parliament set up a
Royal Commission, which was simply a committee of delegates
who were to study, investigate, and report on all aspects of
filmmaking in Australia. By this time there was much concern--
especially on the part of Australian film directors, producers,
distributors, and exhibitors--that the American cinema was in
a position of having a virtual monopoly in the motion picture
industry worldwide, and this in turn was not doing any good
for local films.

A committee of distinguished Australian film producers,
headed by Franklyn Barrett, Raymond Longford, and Arthur
Shirley, appoached the government with proposals calling for,
among other things, the study of the various American corpora-
tions that had been set up in Australia. Also, questions were
raised concerning government quotas, government taxes, and
government tariffs in order to protect Australia's film industry.
One important step was the Censorship of Films Act of 1926,
but this did not end the problems because the act dealt with
certain Australian states rather than all of them.

Unfortunately, the committee wasted much time in traveling all over the country with incessant meetings and interviewing
witnesses. Not until two years after its formation did the Royal

Commission actually begin to make concrete decisions and finally start to take some serious action.

Around this time, the influence of the American film industry was as high as ever, and Australian audiences were
averaging two trips per month to the cinema. American films
were quite popular with Australian audiences, due largely to
the fact that the sheer number of motion pictures made in
Hollywood far ourstripped those made anywhere else. It was
also due to this fact that many Australian actors and actresses
were now migrating to Hollywood, where employment opportun-
ities were far greater than in Australia. Performers such as
Arthur Shirley, Louise Lovely, Enid and Marjorie Bennett,
Rupert Julian, and Lotus Thompson all found steady work in
America, which made for easier employment when some of them
eventually returned to Australia.

Australian cinema just before the sound era in the late
1920's initiated techniques that had been in use in the United
States in order to improve the level of their own productions.
A number of cameramen and other technicians had gone to Hollywood to learn lighting techniques and the like which they brought
back with them, along with writers and producers who learned
the development of creativity concerning film plots, story lines,
and character development. Those Who Love (1926) and The
Far Paradise (1928) were two notable films of the twenties to
use these new methods. Their producers, the three McDonagh
sisters (who were producers of notable Australian features
during this period), saw the aspects necessary to use for
distribution in a worldwide market.

Another praiseworthy film of the period was called The
Kid Stakes by Tal Ordell, which incorporated American production values with Australian events and characterizations.
The film was based on an Australian cartoon strip, Fatty Finn
(which would be made into a film again in 1983). Ordell was an
Australian character actor of stage and motion pictures of
some distinction, although he had directed only one minor film
six years earlier.

Ordell skillfully contrasted the patrician and working
classes, using location scenes to great advantage in this film.
Satire was shown through understatement, and the primarily
childish cast was given to spontaneous rather then studied
acting. Although not an overwhelmingly critical success,

The Kid Stakes nonetheless proved to be popular with the public,
especially children, and it is rather sad and unfortunate to
note that Ordell was never again to direct a motion picture.

The Royal Commission was still busily active, discussing
financing and overseas promotion, distribution, and exporta-
tion of Australian films, most of which during the late 1920s
were suffering from inefficient funding. A good many of
them had to be shot on shoestring budgets with the result
being lower quality. Also, the problems of critical reception of
Austraian films in the U.S. had to be dealt with; Australian
films, primarily due to their plots and subject matter, had a
far greater local than overseas appeal.

During the late 1920s, the coming of sound films signaled
the end to many film production companies and the beginning
for others. As was true with films made in Hollywood and
Great Britian, the first talking pictures made in Australia
were made with partial rather than entire sound tracks. One
of the prominent Australian pioneers in the sound era was
Ray Allsop, who invented certain sound projection equipment
under the title "Raycophone."

Movietone was a company that was functioning internation-
ally and it was with the advent of sound that Australia was
added to its list of production areas (up to that time Movietone
had shown no interest in or ties with Australia). Movietone
was a company that produced newsreel shorts, and although
they had earlier produced newsreels with sound accompani-
ment, they were now producing actual "sound-on-film" material.
Australia's answer to Movietone was locally made newsreels
(which were naturally concerned with news more appropriate
to the country than to the rest of the world) released under
different headings, the two most noteworthy being Cinesound
Review and Herald Newsreel.

Australia was not to escape the Great Depression of the
thirties, which would also have an impact on its motion picture
industry. Following the stock market crash of 1929, unemployment in Australia was at its highest point since before the
First World War, and in a mere three years, would triple.
Combined with economic failure was a higher tax on entertainment, resulting in grossly low profits.

In 1929 production began on a film entitled Showgirl's Luck,

which was directed by Norman Dawn and starred his wife,
Susan Dennis. This was to be Austrialia's first sound motion
picture. Beset by technical as well as financial problems, the
film was not actually completed and released until a year later.

This film, along with two other early sound features Out
of the Shadows and The Cheaters, were entered in a competition
sponsored by the Appeal Board of the Commonwealth Censors
Department; however, they all lost out to a comedy-drama set
during the First World War entitled The Fellers.

A. R. Harwood was the first Australian director to present
two features together: Isle of Intrigue and Spur of the Moment.
Both were filmed in 1931 and released together as a double bill
later in the same year.

However, it was Frank Thring who gave a strong boost to
the early sound film industry in Australia. In 1930 he set up
Efftee Film Corporation, directing a number of these early
sound features himself. Thring succeeded in getting the
government to reduce the import taxes on sound equipment and
recording gear. His first project was a popular comedy entitled A Co-Respondent's Course, which was also unique in
that Thring initiated post-production dubbing over location
shots.

It was Frank Thring who was also responsible for the
success of a series of films which were co-directed by him along
with Pat Hanna, who had had a troupe of performers during
the previous decade called Diggers. This group of performers
was the basis of the 1931 film entitled Diggers, which was the
first of three immensely popular entertainment films. This
was so popular that it led to a sequel, Diggers in Blighty,
made in 1932, which in turn inspired another along the line
called Waltzing Matilda (1933).

Thring began to do a series of short films in a sort of
unified featurette manner, producing nearly one hundred of
them all together. These depicted such subjects as variety
and music hall sketches, vaudeville interludes, speeches from
dignitaries, and just plain recitations from the stage.

Universal Pictures Corporation had set up a branch in
Australia, and the first film to be done there through

the corporation was a remake of The Sentimental Bloke in
1932. This was done in co-operation with Efftee Films. Unlike
its previous version, the film was allocated a large budget
and also had the author, C. J. Dennis, as scriptwriter.

In 1932, Thring followed this up with one of the first of
several very popular musical comedies, His Royal Highness,
which starred the music hall comic George Wallace. This proved
to be such a great success with the movie-going public that
Wallace made two more motion pictures with Thring, the first
being Harmony Row, which was released early in 1934, and
the second A Ticket in Tatts, which was made and released
later in the same year. It was largely the great talent of
Wallace himself, rather than Thring, however, that ensured
the immense financial and popular success of these films.

On Our Selection was also an important film made in Australia in the early sound era (1932). It was a combination of
melodramatic and romantic escapades, along with broad farce.
The film was based on the Steele Rudd stories with the by now
legendary characters of the Rudd family. Directed by Ken G.
Hall, it shattered all previous box-office records; not only did
it run for five years, but it made its backers in excess of
ten times their original investment.

The Squatter's Daughter, made in 1933, was the second
film to be directed by Ken G. Hall. It depended on the dramatic
use of the camera and relied less on dialogue; it had one of the
largest budgets of any Australian film up to that time. The
result was not only a financial success but a critical one as
well.

It was also Frank Thring who led a new campaign by
Australian directors and producers to renew the call for an
Australian film quota in order to fight the Hollywood distribution companies that were once again dealing in the Australian
film market. Recognizing the advantages concerning cultural
and economic importance in the Australian film industry, Thring
invested much of his own money in trying to develop a contin-
gency system, whereby the Australian government could control
the number of foreign films exhibited and imported depending
upon the number of exported Australian films.

An Inquiry Into the Film Industry was then set up in New
South Wales, which turned out to be almost as long winded and

time wasting as had been the Royal Commission several years before. The result was a futility of nonsense, with no action taken and nothing resolved.

Meanwhile, Thring was closing down Efftee in a sort of protest for all the folderol that was going on. Finally in 1935, the government passed an Australian quota, known as the Cinematograph Film Bill, which said there would be no government restriction of theater licenses; no interference in film hire rates, blind booking, block booking, or rejection rates; and, most importantly, a five-year quota on Australian films. Naturally distributors were ecstatic, and Thring decided to move Efftee to Sydney, where unfortunately he died unexpectedly in 1936.

Newsreel footage was still the most widely seen type of motion picture shown in cinemas in the 1930s in Australia. Most of the news agencies that dealt with newsreels were acutely aware of the difficulty in filming news stories. Observing painstaking details and taking public interest and interpretation into consideration were needed when putting them together. These newsreels generally consisted of a number of stories; some were straight news items (horseracing and the like), while others were magazine items, such as novelty acts.

Cinesound News had hired documentarist Frank Hurley throughout the thirties to make films that were commissioned by the government and also Australian industralists. Most of his work at this time consisted of travelogs, which displayed his flair for visual perfection and were quite popular with the public.

After the Quota Act of 1935, National Productions, a subsidiary of National Studios, was established in an effort to create a large-scale independent film industry producing features for the world market as well as to provide advanced studio facilities for independent producers. A staunch ally of the film industry was Bertram Stevens, then Premier of New South Wales. His support stirred optimism which had been lacking in the Australian film industry for some time.

Gaumont-British was one of the biggest names in the British film industry, and the company considered Australia a ground for exploration with their films, thus providing work for Australian technicians and performers in British-Australian co-productions. Also, the Quota Act provided for a guaranteed release of a certain number of Australian films in England.

Gaumont-British sent as a representative to Australia the director Robert Flaherty, who had recently completed Man of Aran in 1934, in order to do research on an upcoming film. He was also to get a feeling for local Australian color and acquaint himself with the customs as well as the people. However, these plans came to nothing when agreements between Gaumont and Australia's National (where Flaherty was supposed to film his project) were broken off.

What eventually did transpire was an agreement between Gaumont-British and National which sent technician Charles Fry to Australia to oversee the finishing of the National Studio completion, accomplished in September of 1935. Also as part of this agreement, the distinguished British actor/producer/ director Miles Mander was sent to Australia to take charge of a production, actually the first at the new National Studio, which was entitled The Flying Doctor and filmed in 1935. Australian director Claude Fleming began work there simultaneously on the film Magic Shoes. This film would mark the debut of British star Peter Finch, who was also to become one of Australia's leading radio personalities during the thirties.

The motion picture industry was struggling along at this point in Australia, due primarily to the Depression; however, the proclamation of the New South Wales Quota Act of 1935 brought renewed hope to Australian film producers.

Throughout 1936, this hope was both reflected and enhanced by the fact that film exhibitors saw an increase of 25 percent of the gross receipts of box office returns (these figures are worldwide as well as Australian). This was the highest level of affluence in more than five years. This new confidence inspired the reconstruction and building of more theaters and cinemas in Australia. There was also a boom in new suburban cinemas which resulted from the fact that Australia had had a massive suburban growth since the 1920s. Crick and Furse was a company of architects in Australia who specialized in cinema construction and renovation. They had already either built or remodeled more than one hundred cinemas in Australia by 1936. In that year alone they built a dozen new cinemas and remodeled more than twice that number.

Nationalism was re-emerging in Australia in the late thirties, and this was reflected in the film industry, especially in the films made by Cinesound. In 1938, Australia celebrated the anniversary of the first European settlers 150 years previously. Newsreels recorded firework displays and re-enactments of the settlement. Frank Hurley filmed a documentary about this event which he called A Nation Is Built. This film was produced on behalf of the New South Wales Government by Cinesound.

Let George Do It was the first in a series of half a dozen comedy features produced by Cinesound Films over the next three years (1938-40). The plot involved an unemployed stagehand who is pursued by gangsters. This film along with the others in the series, used a good deal of cinematic inventiveness, such as a sequence when the hero of the piece foils a bogus conjurer's efforts.

South-African born actor Cecil Kellaway, who had appeared in the Australian film It Isn't Done in 1938, was selected to star as George Chedworth in the popular 1939 production of Mr. Chedworth Steps Out, which also included Peter Finch, who by now was at his apex on the radio.

Gone to the Dogs, Come Up Smiling, and Dad Rudd, M.P. were the last films in the series of comedies for Cinesound, the last film having in its cast Chips Rafferty, who would later become one of the biggest stars of the cinema in Australia. Rafferty starred the following year in a film directed by Charles Chauvel called Forty Thousand Horsemen, which depicted the World War One exploits of three Australian cavalrymen. This was the first Australian film which was to attain true international stature. It also returned its investment in a very short time and proved to be a great morale-booster for the Second World War, which had just begun.

With the outbreak of the Second World War, the motion picture industry in Australia supported the country's stance with an active promotion of recruiting drives, war bonds sales, and austerity loans. Special newsreels were produced on these subjects as well as the subject of national defense. Mobile units were set up providing free viewings to those in the military; also, free distribution was given to propaganda films by government sources. Commercial producers in Australia were to

make a large number of these films during the war for the Department of Information.

The actual number of motion picture feature films made in
Australia during the war was about ten or twelve. Only one,
however, The Rats of Tobruk, made in 1944, directly dealt
with the Australian soldier in battle. It reflected an aware-
ness of the hostilities that ran through nearly all the films
made in Australia at this time, although in this case much more
overtly.

Racing Luck, made in 1941, is a significant Australian
motion picture in that it is one of the very few films to por-
tray average, working-class Australians as credible people
rather than caricatures.

Aside from the normal financial constraints, the Australian
film industry during the war was hurt by a shortage of man-
power (many people connected with all the various aspects of
filmmaking had enlisted in the military services), as well as
by actual deficiencies in the availability of film stock itself.
To help this problem somewhat, a waiver was passed in 1942
that protected employees of the Cinesound and Movietone companies from conscription.

The Department of Information in Australia had been formed
right at the beginning of the war. Its purpose was to coordinate as well as to censor any and all media information released
in Australia that was pertinent to the war. In 1940, the Department of Information formed a National Films Council, which
advised the Department in film distribution, exhibition, and
production. Another offshoot was the Film Division of the
Department of Information, whose function was to coordinate
commercial and governmental film activity; in other words,
propaganda.

Several war correspondents worked with the Department of
Information, and this was the first was department to employ
Australian cinematographers as war correspondents. Director
Frank Hurley was sent in September of 1940 to take charge of
a film crew in the Middle East. Later on, the Australian Air
Force and Army were appointing their own film staff and crews.

Probably the most renowned Australian-made wartime
documentary was the 1944 film Jungle Patrol, narrated by Peter

Finch and highly praised for its authenticity and intensity.
The story was told factually, with no attempt at dramatization,
thus making its realism all the more acute.

Newsreels at this time were naturally taking on a greater
significance. What had once been something of a novelty was
now transformed into a necessity, and newsreel theaters flour-
ished in Australia throughout the war. Some one hundred films
were made during the war under the auspices of the Department of Information, the most noteworthy being dramatized
short films which were commissioned by such producers as
Argosy, Chauvel, and Cinesound.

It was Chauvel who achieved a great success with probably
the most popular wartime film in Australia, The Rats of Tobruk.
This film starred the two most prominent actors in Australia
at the time, Chips Rafferty and Peter Finch. It was a heroic
tribute to the heroes of the jungle and desert warfare, stressing
the Australian's contribution to the war by having the action
in the film depicting the defenses of Tobruk and New Guinea.

Immediately following the war, England's Ealing Studios decided to co-produce some Australian motion pictures. The first
venture was one of the most renowned and distinguished productions, The Overlanders, made in 1946 and starring Chips
Rafferty. The film is an exciting true account of the massive
overland drive of 100,000 head of cattle in 1942 from the
Northern Territory to the Queensland coast because an invasion
of Australia by the Japanese seemed imminent at the time. The
director of this film was Harry Watt, who painstakingly researched
the event with the help of the Australian government. The feelings of insecurity on the part of the cattle drive's members are
established through the blending of documentary style and
action sequences coupled with the crisp narration of Chips
Rafferty's character, Dan McAlpine, the stockman who led the
drive. This was one of the finest Australian films ever, one
which has lost none of its naturalness, fine qualities, and production values over the years. The brilliant photography was
by Osmond Borrodaile.

Sir Charles Kingsford Smith, the hero of the Pacific Flight
of 1928, was chosen as the subject of the 1946 Australian film
Smithy. After extensive screen testing, the part was finally
played by Ron Randell. This film combined Australian patriotic
sentiment with spectacle and Hollywood-type biographical details.

Randell had also starred the same year in the film <u>A Son Is</u>
<u>Born</u>, which included Peter Finch and John McCallum, and
dealt with an ungrateful son and his relationship with his
mother.

In 1947 <u>Bush Christmas</u>, produced and directed by Ralph
Smart, was filmed. It was the first in a series of motion pictures made by the Children's Entertainment Film Division of
Gaumont/British Instructional, which had been formed by Lord
J. Arthur Rank. Once again, Chips Rafferty starred as one
of a trio of horse thieves who are pursued by a group of children into mountain country where they are subsequently
trapped. This was yet another praiseworthy Australian motion
picture; it has a documentary feeling not unlike that of <u>The</u>
<u>Overlanders</u> and remains a favorite with Australian as well as
international audiences to this day. Rafferty himself chose
the children who acted in the film, and he obviously made wise
selections. The relaxed and naturalistic appearance in the
children's performances is evident throughout the film.

<u>Eureka Stockade</u>, made in 1948, was also done by Harry
Watt in association with Ealing Studios. Again Watt immersed
himself in months of researching the true story of the 1854
rebellion of the Eureka Stockade miners. After a frustrating
delay because of the British government's announcement of
its new tax on foreign film imports (which nearly cancelled the
entire project), the film commenced shooting. The film's
budget skyrocketed when one disaster followed another: first
the worst rains in eighty years pushed production schedules
back for weeks on end,. then Chips Rafferty broke several
ribs and later had his hands badly burned while filming.
Added to this was the loss of several cameras and equipment,
the result being that <u>Eureka Stockade</u> had turned into the
most expensive Australian motion picture ever filmed.

Even though <u>Eureka Stockade</u> turned out to be quite costly,
Ealing Films was committed to proceed with their next Australian
co-production, which was to be called <u>Bitter Springs</u>, eventually
completed and released in 1950. This film was directed by Ralph
Smart, who also wrote the screenplay, and starred English
Comedian Tommy Trinder, Chips Rafferty, Gordon Jackson,
Charles Tingwell, and Michael Pate. Jackson, a Scotsman,
is still very active in films and TV in England, while Tingwell
and Pate are currently quite active in Australian films (Pate
having gone to Hollywood where he was cast quite often,

ironically, as a Native American Indian). In this case, as
with Eureka Stockade, severe rainstorms struck the film company, forcing schedule reductions, which led to other com-
promises.

The film industry in Australia during the 1950s was sustained primarily by documentary films. A great many Australian actors, writers, and directors had left Australia for England,
America and the like after the Second World War, thus crippling
the industry in Australia.

It was the documentary film in Australia during the 1950s
that kept the film industry alive. There were still a few feature films being made each year, the majority of which were
co-productions with companies whose main offices or headquar-
ters were located elsewhere (such as Hollywood's M-G-M
Studios). The medium of radio was also reestablished during
this period, and television was introduced. One of the first
successful Australian television series was Long John Silver,
a 26-part program made in 1955 which starred the British actor
Robert Newton (1905-1956), who had created the role of Long
John Silver in the 1950 motion picture Treasure Island. (Newton
had once again portrayed Long John in a feature film version of
Long John Silver in 1954 as well as the television series.)

Three in One (1956) was a highly commended film, winning
a number of prizes at various film festivals throughout the
world. It was comprised of three stories: "Joe Wilson's Mate."
reinforcing the bonding of union solidarity, was based on the
short story "The Union Buries Its Dead," by Henry Lawson;
"The Load of Wood," which was set during the depression of
the 1930s, harkened back to a time of different values; and
"The City," which focused on idealism and the frustrations
of the young Australian urbanites of the 1950s.

Commercials, industrial training films, educational films,
and other sponsored documentaries all experienced greater
distribution and production in the fifties, a time in which regular feature films were on the decline in Australia. Most of
these films were produced by small units on 16-millimeter, which
helped on cost saving as well as screening convenience.

The Department of Information was a forerunner in the new
style of documentary films during the fifties. One of the most
significant films they produced in this period was entitled

Mike and Stefani, made in 1952. The film was an effort to
counter criticism that selection procedures by the immigration
department were not strict enough. This particular film was
based on a true story, in which a Ukrainian couple, separated
during the war, were reunited in a refugee camp in Germany
and subsequently applied for travel permits to Australia.

However, the highlight of the documentary films made under
the Department's auspices in the fifties was undoubtedly The
Queen in Australia, made in 1954. The film was a record of
the Royal Tour of Australia, which also included comments from
ordinary Australian citizens.

Like the Department of Information Film Division, another
surprising phenomenon was the survival of the Waterside
Worker's Federation Film Unit during the 1950s. This unit
produced about a dozen documentaries during this period,
with subjects including worker exploitation, union solidarity,
housing shortages, the need for pensions, etc., all comprised
of left-wing ideology and expressing radical viewpoints.

The Hungry Miles, produced in 1955, was probably the
most noteworthy documentary produced by the Waterside
Worker's Federation Film Unit. It was a chronicle of the history of the Sydney waterfront, using in some scenes several
hundred dock laborers to recreate scenes of mass unemployment
and scuffling for job tickets in a depiction of the Depression of
the thirties, a period in which many of the same people had
been involved. The culmination of the film was an appeal for
greater unity among the harborside workers.

Another economic recession at the end of the fifties brought
about the dissolution of the Waterside Worker's Federation Film
Unit shortly following the completion of its final film, Hewers
of Coal, in 1958. Although screenings of these documentaries
were primarily confined to unions and film societies, they were
well received there and served the purpose for which they
had made.

Weekly newsreels continued to be an important part of
cinema programs in Australia during the fifties. A number of
special newsreels were made during the fifties not as supple-
mental films, but as primary docu-features dealing with such
controversial topics as health, education and welfare, slum conditions, and industrial waste.

Another important issue at this time in Australia, as in other countries, was the growing fear of Communism. This was reflected in newsreels of the period which in turn mirrored the feelings of the Australian people. These feelings could be seen in demonstrations and social unrest which resulted in turmoil and near riots in some areas.

Actor Chips Rafferty and director Lee Robinson formed Southern International Pictures in 1953. Using a new debenture system operated from a series of loans, they were able to produce some noteworthy films, the first being King of the Coral Sea in 1954, followed by Walk into Paradise in 1956, which dealt with a safari and jungle medicine, and sustained an explorer's sense of interest and kept the pace at a high pitch throughout the film. Dust in the Sun, (1958), The Stowaway, (1958), and The Restless and the Damned (1959) were three of the last films made by Southern International. After the failure of these films the company was forced to be liquidated, due largely to the starting of the television industry in Australia and also the general feeling from Rafferty and Lee that there was no future in this endeavor.

Despite the financial failure of Eureka Stockade at the beginning of the decade, British studios were still ready to finance some Australian co-productions. American film companies had also completed one or two films in Australia at the beginning of the 1950s, such as Kangaroo, which starred Peter Lawford, Richard Boone, Maureen O'Hara, Finlay Currie, and Chips Rafferty, and was directed by Lewis Milestone. It was not critically or financially successful.

The British co-productions of the period included Smiley (1956) and its sequel, Smiley Gets a Gun (1958) A Town Like Alice (1956), and Robbery Under Arms (1957). The last, which was based on the novel by Rolfe Bolderwood, starred Peter Finch as Captain Starlight. Immediately following Robbery Under Arms, Finch was selected to star in the film The Shiralee, which had been adapted from the D'Arcy Niland book of the same title. It depicted the story of an Australian swagman named McCauley (Finch) and his "Shiralee" or burden, which in this case happened to be his small daughter. This was a well-received film by both the critics and the public, and Peter Finch always remembered it as one of his favorite motion pictures.

Other notable films of the time were The Siege of Pinchgut (1959); The Summer of the Seventeenth Doll (1959) with Ernest Borgnine, Sir John Mills, Anne Baxter, and Angela Lansbury; On the Beach (1959); and Shadow of the Boomerang (1960).

Another important motion picture of this time period was The Sundowners (1960), starring Robert Mitchum, Deborah Kerr, Peter Ustinov, Chips Rafferty, Glynis Johns, Mervyn Johns, Dina Merrill, John Meillon, Ewen Solon, and Wylie Watson. This film was both a critical and a financial success. The picturesque examples of Australian nature and wildlife enhanced and augmented the story, which had been based on the novel The Sundowners by Jon Cleary. The film captured Australian national sentiment and portrayed domestic intimacy among its characters with conviction. Following The Sundowners, The Bungala Boys (1961) and They Found a Cave (1962) were the only motion pictures to be filmed in Australia until 1965.

In 1965 there was renewed pressure on the government to support the film industry in Australia, subsequently reflected in the 1966 parliamentary election. Filmmakers in the mid and late 1960s in Australia concentrated on underground films, many of which dealt with politics and the war in Vietnam. By the late sixties, Australian films were being financed by other countries in whole or in part, such as Age of Consent (1969), starring James Mason and Helen Mirren; Ned Kelly (1970), starring Mick Jagger as the Australian outlaw; and Adam's Woman (1970), with Beau Bridges, Sir John Mills, Jane Merrow, James Booth, and Andrew Keir.

The year 1971 was probably the turning point in the Australian film industry's resurgence. It was then that two very important films were made signaling the rise in the importance of the film industry. The first was called Outback and starred Gary Bond as a schoolteacher on holiday in the outback. The holiday soon turns into a labyrinthine nightmare of vacuous hospitality and insipid conviviality. Following the loss of his money, Bond joins several locals on a vicious kangaroo hunt, which culminates in a suicide attempt. Also outstanding in the cast were Chips Rafferty (his last role, as he was to drop dead on a street in Sydney the same year), newcomer Jack Thompson, and especially British actor Donald Pleasence as a grotesque alcoholic doctor.

The next film of 1971 was Walkabout, directed by Nicholas Roeg, which depicted the story of two Australian children who are stranded in the desert after their father goes berserk and dies. The story, based on the James Vance Marshall novel, was ably performed by Jenny Agutter, Lucien John, and young aborigine actor David Gulpilil as their guide through the desert.

The success of these films brought with them an entire new wave of actors, directors, and technicians that the Australian film industry had never before seen. Key productions after saw The Adventures of Barry MacKenzie, Libido, Alvin Purple, and Stork. However, even with the success of these films it was becoming apparent that producers of most of these new Australian films were not going to be able to show a profit against their investments merely on local screenings of these films in Australia. A concentrated effort became absolutely vital to achieve overseas sales and worldwide distribution. The Cannes Film Festival provided a vital opportunity for Australian producers to evaluate international market prospects for their films.

It was at the Cannes Film Festival in 1974 that Peter Weir's motion picture The Cars That Ate Paris got enormous critical favor and subsequently opened the door for dealings between Australian and American film companies and distributors.

Between the Wars (1974) was also a successful film made in Australia, depicting the story of a doctor (portrayed by Corin Redgrave, son of Sir Michael Redgrave) who is caught up in the controversial political issues of the Depression era and up to the Second World War. The reviews of this film were enormously favorable. Critics praised the film for its detached perspective and its involved and generally well-handled character interpretations.

Mad Dog Morgan, made in 1976 and starring Dennis Hopper, Jack Thompson, and David Gulpilil, along with Picnic at Hanging Rock (also 1976) gave a further boost to the reputation of the re-emerging Australian film industry. Picnic at Hanging Rock is an eerie tale of the disappearance of several schoolgirls and a teacher in 1900. It was a major box-office hit in Australia and Europe.

The Last Wave, made in 1977 and starring Richard Chamberlain, was another venture into the mystical by director Peter Weir. The story dealt with a lawyer (Chamberlain) defending an Aborigine (David Gulpilil). The lawyer discovers that an ancient tribe living in caves just outside Sydney are in fact guardians of prehistoric wall paintings that deal with destruction by a gigantic tidal wave. The clashes of cultures and races leaves Chamberlain with his own premonition of the cataclysm.

My Brilliant Career (1979), based on the novel by Miles Franklin, was another significant Australian film which also did a great deal in the way of international film distribution. It is a love story about a young woman (excellently portrayed by Judy Davis) divided between the stirrings of passion and her need for self-fulfillment.

The next Australian film of note is undoubtedly one of the best ever: Breaker Morant made in 1980 and starring Edward Woodward (now famous as television's "The Equalizer" Robert McCall) Bryan Brown, Jack Thompson, and Lewis Fitzgerald, along with a brilliant supporting cast including John Waters, Charles Tingwell, Rod Mullinar, Terence Donovan, Ray Meagher, and Vincent Ball. It is the true story of three members of the Bushveldt Carbineers (Woodward, Brown, and Fitzgerald) on trial in 1901 during the Boer War for allegedly murdering Boer prisoners. The trio are tried by a clearly biased military tribunal, which has decided to make an example of them for political reasons.

Bryan Brown, who won critical acclaim for Breaker Morant, went on the following year to star with Helen Morse and Gordon Jackson in a stirring remake of A Town Like Alice and later also had a role in The Thorn Birds.

Another first-rate film was Gallipoli made in 1981 and directed by Peter Weir. It depicted the story of two young Australians (Mel Gibson and Mark Lee) who take part in what most Australians consider their most famous historical moment, the landing of troops at Gallipoli in 1915 during the First World War. Gallipoli received excellent reviews all over the world and was quite successful.

The Man from Snowy River, and The Year of Living Dangerously were two significant Australian films made in 1982.

The first was based on the famous epic poem by A.B. Patterson, while the latter dealt with an Australian journalist in Indonesia.

Phar Lap (1983) told the true story of the famous Australian racehorse and its mysterious death. The story appealed to old and young alike. It was shot on a tight budget and schedule and rekindled the nation's fascination with the horse that had captured the imagination of millions during the Depression era.

In the last couple of years the short film and the documentary film has gone through a rich period in Australia, and in many cases these are superior to feature films in quality. For this, much credit can be taken by the Creative Development Branch and Women's Film Fund of the Australian Film Commission. It is to be hoped that some of the talented artists that have been concentrating in this area will also turn to the feature film scene.

Australian films have made great strides in the past fifteen years, but state and federal government funding is still an important role in the film industry there. However, with the recent worldwide success of films like Crocodile Dundee (1986), starring Paul Hogan as an Australian hunter in New York City, which smashed all box-office records in Australia, it would certainly appear that the Australian film industry will keep producing films not only financially successful, but also films of great and lasting quality.

FILM ACTORS AND ACTRESSES

DOROTHY ALISON (1925-)

Australian supporting actress of stage, screen, and television; long in England. Former secretary.

Eureka Stockade	1948
The Sons of Matthew	1949
Mandy	1952
Turn the Key Softly	1953
The Maggie	1954
Child's Play	1954
The Purple Plain	1954
Companions in Crime	1955
The Silken Affair	1956
The Feminine Touch	1956
Reach for the Sky	1956
The Long Arm	1956
The Scamp	1957
Interpol	1957
The Man Upstairs	1958
Life in Emergency Ward Ten	1959
The Nun's Story	1959
Two Living One Dead	1961
The Prince and the Pauper	1962
Georgy Girl	1966
Pretty Polly	1967
See No Evil	1971

The Amazing Mr. Blunden	1972
Dr. Jekyll and Sister Hyde	1972
Baxter	1973
En Vandring I Solen	1976
Sister Dora	1977
Eustace and Hilda	1977
A Walk in the Sun	1978
Forgive Our Foolish Ways	1980
The Errand	1981
A Town Like Alice	1981
Invitation to the Wedding	1982
Return of the Soldier	1982
The Winds of Jarrah	1983
The Schippan Mystery	1984
A Fortunate Life	1986
Tusitala	1986

HARRY ALLEN (1883-1951)

Australian character and supporting actor in Hollywood; also on stage.

The Last Moment	1923
The Enchanted Cottage	1924
Corporal Kate	1926
Ella Cinders	1926
The Silent Hero	1927
The Scorcher	1927
Turkish Delight	1927
The Adorable Cheat	1928
Two Lovers	1928
The Singapore Mutiny	1928
Sweet Sixteen	1928
Strange Cargo	1929
In Old California	1929
The Dawn Patrol	1930
Headin' North	1930
Hell Harbour	1930
Hell's Island	1930
Sunny	1930
Second Honeymoon	1930
Chances	1931
Rich Man's Folly	1931
Texas Pioneers	1932

The Fourth Horseman	1933
Bombay Mail	1934
Silver Streak	1935
Anna Karenina	1935
The White Angel	1936
The White Legion	1936
California Straight Ahead	1937
Outside of Paradise	1938
The Little Princess	1939
Moon Over Burma	1940
Buckskin Frontier	1943
Forever and a Day	1943
The Hour Before the Dawn	1944
The Lodger	1944
The Swordsman	1947
Thunder in the Valley	1947
Bob, Son of Battle	1948

JACK ALLEN

Sometimes bearded Australian supporting actor of occasional films and TV.

Ned Kelly	1970
Sunstruck	1972
And Millions Will Die	1973
Inn of the Damned	1974
House of Mortal Sin	1975
Barney	1976
Lost in the Wild	1977
The Odd Angry Shot	1979
Sam	1980
The Dismissal	1983
Around the World in 80 Ways	1986
The Last Frontier	1986
Colour in the Creek	1987

GLEN ALYN (1913-)

Australian supporting actress and occasional leading lady of the thirties, also on stage (from 1920).

| Head of the Family | 1933 |

Mayfair Girl	1933
Trouble in Store	1934
Grand Finale	1936
It's in the Bag	1936
Gypsy	1937
Don't Get Me Wrong	1937
The Perfect Crime	1937
Ship's Concert	1937
The Windmill	1937
Mayfair Melody	1937
You Live and Learn	1937
The Dark Stairway	1938
The Singing Cop	1938
Sweet Devil	1938
Simply Terrific	1938
It's in the Blood	1938
Thank Evans	1938
The Ware Case	1938
A Window in London	1939
Law and Disorder	1940
Old Mother Riley Joins Up	1940
There's Always a Thursday	1957

DAME JUDITH ANDERSON (1898-   )

Distinguished, formidable Australian actress of stage (since 1915), screen and television, sometimes seen in sinister or menacing roles. Long in U.S. TV series: Santa Barbara (1984-   ).

Madame of the Jury	1930
Judith Anderson	1932
Blood Money	1933
Macbeth	1937
Forty Little Mothers	1940
Rebecca	1940
Free and Easy	1941
King's Row	1941
Lady Scarface	1941
All Through the Night	1942
Edge of Darkness	1943
Stage Door Canteen	1943
Laura	1944
And Then There Were None	1945

Diary of a Chambermaid	1946
Specter of the Rose	1946
Strange Love of Martha Ivers	1946
Pursued	1947
The Red House	1947
Tycoon	1947
The Furies	1950
The Silver Chord	1951
Come of Age	1953
Jane Eyre	1953
Salome	1953
Black Chiffon	1954
Christmas Story	1954
Yesterday's Magic	1954
Louise	1955
Virtue	1955
The Senora	1955
Creative Impulse	1955
Circular Staircase	1956
The Ten Commandments	1956
Cradle Song	1956
Caesar and Cleopatra	1956
The Clouded Image	1957
Abbey, Julia, and the Seven Pet Cows	1958
Cat on a Hot Tin Roof	1958
The Bridge of the San Luis Rey	1958
The Moon and Sixpence	1959
Second Happiest Day	1959
Medea	1959
Cinderfella	1960
Macbeth	1960
To the Sounds of Trumpets	1960
Millionaire's Might	1960
Why Bother to Knock?	1961
Macbeth	1966
Elizabeth the Queen	1968
The File on Devlin	1969
Hamlet	1970
A Man Called Horse	1970
The Borrowers	1973
Inn of the Damned	1974
The Underground Man	1974
The Chinese Prime Minister	1975
Medea	1983
Star Trek III: The Search for Spock	1984
The Thrill of Genius	1985

BASIL APPLEBY

Character actor who was seen in some films of the 1940s and
1950s; also director.

Pimpernel Smith	1941
49th Parallel	1941
The End of the River	1947
The Weaker Sex	1948
Hi Jinks in Society	1949
No Highway	1951
Heights of Danger	1953
Stryker of the Yard	1953
The Black Knight	1954
Betrayed	1954
The Dam Busters	1955
Above Us the Waves	1955
Reach for the Sky	1956

ALEXANDER ARCHDALE

Australian character actor who has made sporadic film appearances.

Lucky Days	1935
House of Darkness	1948
Floodtide	1949
His Majesty O'Keefe	1954
Under the Black Flag	1957
Fiend Without a Face	1958
The Scapegoat	1959
The Headless Ghost	1959
A Touch of Larceny	1959
Village of the Damned	1960
Invasion Quartet	1961
Marriage of Convenience	1961
Born to Run	1977
Newsfront	1978
Night of the Prowler	1979
The Killing of Angel Street	1981
Colour in the Creek	1987

DAVID ARGUE

Australian supporting and sometimes leading actor of films of
the 80s; also on television.

Gallipoli	1981
Midnite Spares	1982
The Return of Captain Invincible	1982
Going Down	1983
The Coca Cola Kid	1984
Razorback	1984
BMX Bandits	1984
Melvin, Son of Alvin	1984
Stanley	1985
Neil Lynne	1985
Backlash	1986
Pandemonium	1987

OSCAR ASCHE (1871-1936)

Australian supporting actor of the 1930s; primarily seen on
the stage.

Kismet	1914
Don Quixote	1933
My Lucky Star	1933
Two Hearts in Waltz Time	1934
Scrooge	1935
Private Secretary	1935
Eliza Comes to Stay	1936
Robber Symphony	1936

EDWARD ASHLEY (1904-)

Australian leading actor of the 30s who went to Hollywood and
was given auxiliary parts. Also on stage and (latterly) television. Formerly married to Nora Swinburne.

Men of Steel	1932
Timbuctoo	1933
Old Faithful	1935
White Lilac	1935
Under Proof	1936

Saturday Night Revue	1937
Underneath the Arches	1937
The Villiers Diamond	1938
Spies of the Air	1939
Pride and Prejudice	1940
Bitter Sweet	1940
Sky Murder	1940
Gallant Sons	1940
Maisie Was a Lady	1941
Come Live With Me	1941
You're Telling Me	1942
The Black Swan	1942
Love Honor and Goodbye	1945
The Madonna	1946
Nocturne	1946
Dick Tracy vs. Gruesome	1947
The Other Love	1947
Gay Blades	1947
Tarzan & the Mermaids	1948
Dick Tracy's Amazing Adventure	1949
Tarzan's Peril	1951
Tarzan & the Jungle Queen	1951
Macao	1952
El Alamein	1953
Elephant Walk	1954
Desert Patrol	1954
Volturio Investigates	1954
The Court Jester	1956
Darby's Rangers	1958
King Rat	1965
Herbie Rides Again	1973
Genesis II	1973
Won Ton Ton	1976

ROSALIND ATKINSON (1900-1978)

New Zealand character actress long on stage; films rare but
memorable.

Tomorrow We Live	1936
Tom Jones	1963
The Pumpkin Eater	1964

FRANK BAKER (1894-1980)

Australian supporting and, latterly, character actor of films
and TV, long in Hollywood.

The Diamond Bandit	1924
Lash of the Whip	1924
Red Blood and Blue	1925
Scar Hanan	1925
The Gallant Fool	1926
Wolf's Trail	1927
The Bushranger	1928
Call of the Heart	1928
A Million for Love	1929
The New Adventures of Tarzan	1935
Mary of Scotland	1936
The Baroness & the Butler	1938
Four Men and a Prayer	1938
Tarzan & the Green Goddess	1938
Arrest Bulldog Drummond	1939
A Chump at Oxford	1940
Two Rode Together	1961
Donovan's Reef	1963
Defiance	1975

VINCENT BALL (1924-)

Cheerful Australian character player who was most active in
the 1950s and 1960s; also on television.

Interrupted Journey	1949
Stop Press Girl	1949
Warning to Wantons	1949
The Blue Lagoon	1949
Come Dance with Me	1950
London Entertains	1951
Talk of a Million	1951
Encore	1952
The Drayton Case	1953
Dangerous Voyage	1954
Devil's Point	1954
The Dark Stairway	1954
The Black Rider	1954
The Blue Peter	1955

Stolen Time	1955
John and Julie	1955
The Big Fish (voice)	1955
The Baby and the Battleship	1956
A Town Like Alice	1956
Secret of the Forest	1956
Face in the Night	1957
Robbery Under Arms	1957
Blood of the Vampire	1958
Sea of Sand	1958
Danger Within	1959
Summer of the Seventeenth Doll	1959
Identity Unknown	1960
Feet of Clay	1960
Dead Lucky	1960
Dentist in the Chair	1960
Nearly a Nasty Accident	1961
The Middle Course	1961
Highway to Battle	1961
Very Important Person	1961
A Matter of WHO	1962
Carry On Cruising	1962
Echo of Diana	1963
Mouse On the Moon	1963
Follow That Camel	1967
Where Eagles Dare	1968
Oh What a Lovely War	1969
Not Tonite Darling	1971
Clinic Xclusive	1972
Deathcheaters	1976
Demolition	1977
The Irishman	1978
Alison's Birthday	1979
Time Lapse	1980
Breaker Morant	1980
Deadline	1981
The Southern Cross	1982
Learned Friends	1982
Phar Lap	1983
The Highest Honour	1984
Flight into Hell	1985
Butterfly Island	1985
Double Skulls	1986
The Year My Voice Broke	1987
Anzacs	1987

RAY BARRETT (1926-   )

Australian leading man long popular on British television; films
occasional. TV series: The Troubleshooters (1966-71).

The Sundowners	1960
Mix Me a Person	1962
Jigsaw	1962
Time to Remember	1962
Touch of Death	1962
Moment of Decision	1962
To Have and to Hold	1963
80,000 Suspects	1963
Valley of the Kings	1964
The Reptile	1965
Thunderbirds Are Go	1966
Just Like a Woman	1966
Revenge	1971
The Amorous Milkman	1974
The Hostages	1975
No Room to Run	1976
Let the Balloon Go	1977
Don's Party	1978
The Chant of Jimmie Blacksmith	1979
The Timeless Land	1980
Goodbye Paradise	1981
A Dangerous Summer	1982
A Shifting Dreaming	1982
The Wild Duck	1983
Waterfront	1983
Aussie Assault (voice)	1984
Where the Green Ants Dream	1984
Conference-Ville	1984
No Name No Pack Drill	1985
The Empty Beach	1985
Comedy	1985
The Last Bastion	1985
Rebel	1985
Frenchman's Farm	1986
Tusitala	1986
The Challenge	1987
Running Wild	1987
As Time Goes By	1987

MONA BARRIE (1909-   )

Australian leading lady and second lead of Hollywood films,
generally seen in graceful roles; also on stage.

Sleepers East	1933
The House of Connelly	1934
Carolina	1934
One Night of Love	1934
Charlie Chan in London	1934
Such Women Are Dangerous	1934
I'll Fix It	1934
Mystery Woman	1935
The Melody Lingers On	1935
King of Burlesque	1936
A Message to Garcia	1936
Love on the Run	1936
Mountain Justice	1937
I Met Him in Paris	1937
Something to Sing About	1937
Love, Honor and Behave	1938
Men Are Such Fools	1938
Say It in French	1938
I Take This Woman	1940
Lady with Red Hair	1940
When Ladies Meet	1941
Ellery Queen & the Murder Ring	1941
Never Give a Sucker an Even Break	1941
Skylark	1941
Today I Hang	1942
The Road to Happiness	1942
Cairo	1942
Syncopation	1942
The Strange Case of Dr. Rx	1942
One Dangerous Night	1943
Storm Over Lisbon	1944
Just Before Dawn	1946
I Cover the Big Town	1947
Cass Timberlane	1947
Strange Fascination	1952
Plunder of the Sun	1953

JOHN BATTEN (1905-   )

New Zealand leading man and second lead, also on stage and
in Hollywood.

The Godless Girl	1927
Back Stage	1927
Her Great Ambition	1928
Battle of the Sexes	1928
Under the Greenwood Tree	1929
The Great Game	1930
Men Like These	1931
The Love Waltz	1931
The Wonderful Story	1932
As Good As New	1933
Call Me Mame	1933
High Finance	1933
The Church Mouse	1934
For Those in Peril	1944

MAY BEATTY (1881-1945)

New Zealand character actress of stage and screen in Hollywood.

The Benson Murder Case	1930
The Boudior Diplomat	1930
Ex-Flame	1931
The Little Minister	1934
Horse Play	1934
Night Life of the Gods	1935
Becky Sharp	1935
Mad Love	1935
Here Comes the Band	1935
The Girl Who Came Back	1935
Bonnie Scotland	1935
Sylvia Scarlett	1936
Little Lord Fauntleroy	1936
Show Boat	1936
Private Number	1936
Lloyds of London	1936
Call It a Day	1937
Four Days' Wonder	1937
She Loved a Fireman	1937
If I Were King	1938

The Women	1939
Eternally Yours	1939
We Are Not Alone	1939
Adventures of Sherlock Holmes	1939
Union Pacific	1939
Queen of the Mob	1940
Pride and Prejudice	1940
My Son My Son	1940
I Wake Up Screaming	1941
The Crystal Ball	1943
Lassie Come Home	1943
Forever and a Day	1943

BRUCE BEEBY (1923-)

Australian supporting performer of the fifties and sixties;
also on television.

Women of Twilight	1953
The Intruder	1953
The Limping Man	1953
Front Page Story	1954
Malaga	1954
The Golden Link	1954
Radio Cab Murder	1954
Profile	1954
Time Is My Enemy	1954
The Teckman Mystery	1954
A Kid for Two Farthings	1955
Murder of a Ham	1955
Impulse	1955
Man in the Road	1956
Child in the House	1956
Stranger in Town	1957
The Shiralee	1957
Smiley Gets a Gun	1958
Pit of Darkness	1961
Payroll	1961
Serena	1962
A Matter of WHO	1962
It's All Happening	1963
Devil Ship Pirates	1964
Midas Run	1969
Wuthering Heights	1970

ENID BENNETT (1895-1969)

Australian actress in Hollywood who began in silents and played
smaller roles with the advent of sound. Sister of Marjorie
Bennett.

Princess in the Dark	1917
The Biggest Show on Earth	1918
The Vamp	1918
Fuss and Feathers	1918
The Hunted Bedroom	1919
Stepping Out	1919
The Woman and the Suitcase	1920
Hairpins	1920
Her Husband's Friend	1921
Keeping Up With Lizzie	1921
Silk Hosiery	1921
Robin Hood	1922
The Bootlegger's Daughter	1922
Scandalous Tongues	1922
The Bad Man	1923
Courtship of Miles Standish	1923
Strangers of the Night	1923
Your Friend and Mine	1923
The Sea Hawk	1924
The Red Lily	1924
A Fool's Awakening	1925
A Woman's Heart	1926
The Wrong Mr. Wright	1927
Good Medicine	1929
Skippy	1931
Waterloo Bridge	1931
Sooky	1931
Intermezzo	1938
Meet Dr. Christian	1939
A Love Story	1939
Strike Up the Band	1940

MARJORIE BENNETT (1895-1982)

Australian character actress long in Hollywood; also extensively
seen on television. Sister of Enid Bennett.

Dressed to Kill	1946

Monsieur Verdoux	1947
June Bride	1948
Perfect Strangers	1950
Too Dangerous to Live	1950
Two Flags West	1950
The Man Who Cheated Himself	1951
Limelight	1952
Rock Against the Sea	1953
Riccochet Romance	1954
Sabrina	1954
The Young at Heart	1955
The Cobweb	1955
Strange Intruder	1956
Autumn Leaves	1956
Home Before Dark	1958
The Rat Race	1960
The Chase	1960
A Thunder of Drums	1961
101 Dalmatians (voice)	1961
Summer and Smoke	1961
Kick the Can	1962
Sail a Crooked Ship	1962
Whatever Happened to Baby Jane?	1962
Four for Texas	1963
The Man from Galveston	1963
Saintly Sinners	1963
Promises Promises	1963
No Time Like the Past	1963
Mary Poppins	1964
My Fair Lady	1964
Three Nuts in Search of a Bolt	1964
What a Way to Go!	1964
The Family Jewels	1965
The Night Walker	1965
36 Hours	1965
Billy the Kid vs. Dracula	1966
Quick Before it Melts	1966
Games	1967
Coogan's Bluff	1968
The Love God	1969
Calliope	1971
Getting Away from It All	1972
Stacey	1973
Carley Varrick	1973
Mother, Jugs, and Speed	1976

Sherlock Holmes in New York	1976
The North Avenue Irregulars	1979
Better Late Than Never	1979

GEORGE BERANGER (1895-1973)

Australian leading man of silents and later character actor in Hollywood; also a stage actor and director.

Birth of a Nation	1915
The Stab	1915
The Half-Breed	1916
Flirting With Fate	1916
Pillars of Society	1916
Manhattan Madness	1916
The Good-Bad Man	1916
Should She Have Told?	1916
In the Dead of Night	1916
Mixed Blood	1916
Those Without Sin	1917
Sandy	1918
A Bum Bomb	1918
The Leopardess	1923
Dulcy	1923
The Bright Shawl	1923
The Extra Girl	1923
Ashes of Vengeance	1923
Tiger Rose	1923
The Man Life Passed By	1923
Beau Brummel	1924
Grounds for Divorce	1925
Beauty and the Bad Man	1925
Are Parents People?	1925
A Woman's Faith	1925
The Man in Blue	1925
Confessions of a Queen	1925
The Grand Duchess & the Waiter	1926
So This Is Paris	1926
The Bat	1926
Miss Brewster's Millions	1926
The Popular Sin	1926
Eagle of the Sea	1926
Fig Leaves	1926
The Lady of the Harem	1926

Altars of Desire	1927
Paradise For Two	1927
If I Were Single	1927
The Small Bachelor	1927
Powder My Back	1928
Beware of Bachelors	1928
5 & 10 Cent Annie	1928
Stark Mad	1929
Strange Cargo	1929
The Glad Rag Doll	1929
Lilies of the Field	1930
The Boudoir Diplomat	1930
Annabell's Affairs	1931
Surrender	1931
Ladies of the Jury	1931
Mama Loves Papa	1933
Young and Beautiful	1934
Kiss and Make Up	1934
Dangerous	1935
The Pay-Off	1935
The Story of Louis Pasteur	1936
Snowed Under	1936
Love Before Breakfast	1936
The Noise	1936
Walking on Air	1936
Down the Stretch	1936
Colleen	1936
Hot Money	1936
The King of Hockey	1937
Cafe Metropole	1937
Wake Up and Live	1937
I'll Take Romance	1937
Hollywood Roundup	1937
Gilding the Lily	1938
Beauty for the Asking	1939
He Stayed for Breakfast	1940
Our Wife	1941
She Knows All the Answers	1941
Over My Dead Body	1942
Saratoga Trunk	1945
Nightmare Alley	1947
Unfaithfully Yours	1948
Road House	1948
Dancing in the Dark	1949

BILLY BEVAN (1887-1957)

Australian character star and singer of stage and films, long
in Hollywood.

Let Er Go	1920
The Quack Doctor	1920
It's a Boy	1920
My Goodness	1920
Love, Honor and Behave	1920
A Fireside Brewer	1920
Small Town Idol	1921
Be Reasonable	1921
By Heck	1921
Astray from Steerage	1921
The Duck Hunter	1922
On Patrol	1922
Oh Daddy	1922
Gymnasium Jim	1922
Ma and Pa	1922
When Summer Comes	1922
Crossroads of New York	1922
Nip and Tuck	1923
Sinbad the Sailor	1923
The Extra Girl	1923
One Spooky Night	1924
Wall Street Blues	1924
Lilies of the Field	1924
Wandering Waistlines	1924
Cannonball Express	1924
The White Sin	1924
Honeymoon Hardships	1925
Giddap	1925
The Lion's Whiskers	1925
Butter Fingers	1925
Skinners in Silk	1925
Super-Hooper-Dyne Lizzies	1925
Sneezing Beezers	1925
The Iron Nag	1925
Over There-Abouts	1925
From Rags to Britches	1925
Whispering Whiskers	1926
Trimmed in Gold	1926
Circus Today	1926
Wandering Willies	1926

Hayfoot, Strawfoot	1926
Fight Night	1926
Muscle Bound Music	1926
Ice Cold Cocoa	1926
A Sea Dog's Tale	1926
Hubby's Quiet Little Game	1926
Masked Mamas	1926
Hoboken to Hollywood	1926
The Divorce Dodger	1926
Flirty Four-Flushers	1926
Should Sleepwalkers Marry?	1927
Peaches and Plumbers	1927
Small Town Princess	1927
The Bull Fighter	1927
Cured in the Excitement	1927
The Golf Nut	1927
Gold Diggers of Weepah	1927
Easy Pickings	1927
The Beach Club	1928
The Best Man	1928
The Bicycle Flirt	1928
His Unlucky Night	1928
Caught in the Kitchen	1928
Motorboat Mamas	1928
Motoring Mamas	1928
Hubby's Latest Alibi	1928
Hubby's Weekend Trip	1928
The Lion's Roar	1928
His New Steno	1928
Riley the Cop	1928
Calling Hubby's Bluff	1929
Button My Back	1929
Foolish Husbands	1929
Pink Pajamas	1929
Don't Get Jealous	1929
High Voltage	1929
Sky Hawk	1929
Scotch	1930
Journey's End	1930
For the Love O' Lil	1930
Temptation	1930
Peacock Alley	1930
Transatlantic	1931
Sky Devils	1931
Spot on the Rug	1932

Honeymoon Beach	1932
Silent Witness	1932
Vanity Fair	1932
Payment Deferred	1932
Honeymoon Beach (short)	1932
Alice in Wonderland	1933
Big Squeal	1933
Looking Forward	1933
The Midnight Club	1933
Too Much Harmony	1933
A Study in Scarlet	1933
Cavalcade	1933
Luxury Liner	1933
Peg O' My Heart	1933
The Way to Love	1933
The Lost Patrol	1934
Shock	1934
Caravan	1934
Limehouse Blues	1934
Mystery Woman	1935
Black Sheep	1935
The Last Outpost	1935
A Tale of Two Cities	1935
Song and Dance Man	1936
Lloyds of London	1936
Private Number	1936
Dracula's Daughter	1936
Piccadilly Jim	1936
God's Country and the Woman	1936
Slave Ship	1937
Another Dawn	1937
The Sheik Steps Out	1937
The Wrong Road	1937
Bringing Up Baby	1938
Mysterious Mr. Moto	1938
Girl of the Golden West	1938
Shadows Over Shanghai	1938
Captain Fury	1939
Let Freedom Ring	1939
Grand Jury Secrets	1939
We Are Not Alone	1939
Arrest Bulldog Drummond	1939
The Earl of Chicago	1940
The Long Voyage Home	1940
Tim Pan Alley	1940

Shining Victory	1941
Dr. Jekyll and Mr. Hyde	1941
Confirm or Deny	1941
Scotland Yard	1941
Mrs. Miniver	1942
The Man Who Wouldn't Die	1942
London Blackout Murders	1942
Counter Espionage	1942
Appointment in Berlin	1943
Forever and a Day	1943
Return of the Vampire	1943
Young and Willing	1943
The Lodger	1944
National Velvet	1944
The Invisible Man's Revenge	1944
South of Dixie	1944
The Picture of Dorian Gray	1945
Tonight and Every Night	1945
Cluny Brown	1946
Devotion	1946
Terror By Night	1946
Moss Rose	1947
It Had to Be You	1947
The Swordsman	1947
The Black Arrow	1948
Let's Live a Little	1948
The Secret of St. Ives	1949
The Secret Garden	1949
Rogues of Sherwood Forest	1950
Fortunes of Captain Blood	1950

JON BLAKE

Australian leading man seen in occasional films and on television.

Force Ten from Navarone	1978
Something Wicked	1981
Early Frost	1982
Freedom	1983
The Lighthorsemen	1987
Anzacs	1987

GRAEME BLUNDELL

Australian leading man of films and television.

Stork	1974
Alvin Purple	1974
Alvin Purple Rides Again	1975
Three Old Friends	1975
Don's Party	1976
Mad Dog Morgan	1976
Weekend of Shadows	1978
The Odd Angry Shot	1979
Kostas	1980
Pacific Banana	1981
The Best of Friends	1982
Doctors and Nurses	1983
Melvin, Son of Alvin	1984
Australian Dream	1985
Those Dear Departed	1987
Vietnam	1987
The Year My Voice Broke	1987

SIDNEY BRACEY (1877-1942)

Australian character actor of stage and screen in Hollywood, equally active in silent and sound films alike.

Zudora	1914
The Invisible Ray	1920
Amateur Devil	1921
The Outside Women	1921
Passion Fruit	1921
Crazy to Marry	1921
The March Hare	1921
Morals	1921
Manslaughter	1922
The Dictator	1922
Radio King	1922
Is Matrimony a Failure?	1922
Midnight	1922
One Wonderful Night	1922
Merry-Go-Round	1923
Nobody's Bride	1923
Crooked Alley	1923

The Wild Party	1923
Social Buccaneer	1923
Ruggles of Red Gap	1923
Being Respectable	1924
The Divine Right	1924
Her Night of Romance	1924
So This Is Marriage	1924
Why Men Leave Home	1924
Her Market Value	1925
The Merry Widow	1925
Wandering Footsteps	1925
Slave of Fashion	1925
A Man 4 Square	1926
Mystery Club	1926
The Black Bird	1926
My Official Wife	1926
You Never Know Women	1926
Birds of Prey	1927
Painting the Town	1927
The 13th Juror	1927
Woman on Trial	1927
Show People	1928
Haunted House	1928
The Camera Man	1928
Queen Kelly	1928
Wedding Night	1928
Win That Girl	1928
Home James	1928
Man-Made Women	1928
His Captive Woman	1929
Sioux Blood	1929
The Bishop Murder Case	1929
Second Floor Mystery	1930
Anybody's Woman	1930
Outside the Law	1930
Monte Carlo	1930
Free Love	1930
Redemption	1930
What a Bozo	1931
Thundering Tenor	1931
The Avenger	1931
Parlor, Bedroom and Bath	1931
The Lion and the Lamb	1931
Dangerous Affair	1931
Subway Express	1931

Shanghaied Love	1931
The Deceiver	1931
The Monster Walks	1932
The Greeks Had a Word for Them	1932
Tangled Destinies	1932
No More Orchids	1932
Little Orphan Annie	1932
Flying Down to Rio	1933
The Intruder	1933
Corruption	1933
Broken Dreams	1933
The Poor Rich	1934
The Ninth Guest	1934
Les Miserables	1935
I've Been Around	1935
Anna Karenina	1935
Magnificent Obsession	1936
Second Childhood	1936
Sutter's Gold	1936
Isle of Fury	1936
The Preview Murder Mystery	1936
The Firefly	1937
Three Smart Boys	1937
Mr. Chump	1938
The Dawn Patrol	1938
The Baroness and the Butler	1938
Merrily We Live	1938
Mr. Bill	1938
Espionage Agent	1939
On Trial	1939
Smashing the Money Ring	1939
Everybody's Hobby	1939
Sweepstakes Winner	1939
Torchy Runs for Mayor	1939
British Intelligence	1940
My Love Came Back	1940
Devil's Island	1940
Tugboat Annie Sails Again	1940
Dark Victory	1941
Bullets for O'Hara	1941
Scotland Yard	1941
Shadows on the Stairs	1941
The Gay Sisters	1942
The Body Disappears	1942

BRYAN BROWN (1947-)

Personable, good-looking Australian leading man of films and
television; married to Rachel Ward.

Love Letters from Teralba Road	1977
The Irishman	1978
Money Movers	1978
Newsfront	1978
Palm Beach	1979
The Odd Angry Shot	1979
Weekend of Shadows	1979
The Promotion of Mr. Smith	1980
Third Person Plural	1980
Cathy's Child	1980
The Chant of Jimmie Blacksmith	1980
Stir	1980
Breaker Morant	1980
A Town Like Alice	1981
The Winter of Our Dreams	1982
Far East	1982
The Thorn Birds	1982
Undercover	1983
Give My Regards to Broad Street	1983
Eureka Stockade	1983
Kim	1984
No Names No Pack Drill	1984
The Empty Beach	1984
Return to Eden	1984
Bones	1985
The Shiralee	1985
Parker	1985
F/X	1985
Taipan	1986
The Umbrella Woman	1986
Rebel	1986
The Good Wife	1986
Gorilla in the Mist	1987
Cocktail	1987

NANCY BROWN (1910-)

Australian actress of stage (from 1926) and several films of
the thirties.

Maid of the Mountains	1932
Facing the Music	1933
A Southern Maid	1933
Red Wagon	1934

CORAL BROWNE (1913-   )

Australian character actress, also on stage, often seen in wealthy or sophisticated roles. Married to Vincent Price (1911-   ). TV series: Time Express (1979).

Charing Cross Road	1935
Line Engaged	1935
Guilty Melody	1936
The Amateur Gentleman	1936
We're Going to Be Rich	1938
Black Limelight	1938
Yellow Sands	1938
The Nursemaid Who Disappeared	1939
Let George Do It	1940
Piccadilly Incident	1946
The Courtneys of Curzon Street	1947
Kathy's Love Affair	1952
Beautiful Stranger	1954
Auntie Mame	1958
The Roman Spring of Mrs. Stone	1961
Go to Blazes	1962
Tamahine	1963
Dr. Crippen	1964
Night of the Generals	1966
The Legend of Lylah Clare	1968
The Killing of Sister George	1968
Charley's Aunt	1969
The Ruling Class	1972
Theatre of Blood	1973
The Drowning Pool	1975
Xanadu (voice)	1980
Eleanor, First Lady of the World	1982
An Englishman Abroad	1983
American Dreamer	1984
Dream Child	1986

TOM BURLINSON

Youthful Australian leading man who graduated to films through
TV.

Kirby's Company	1977
Yes, What!	1978
Glenview High	1979
Revenge	1980
The Man from Snowy River	1982
Phar Lap	1983
Eureka Stockade	1984
Flesh and Blood	1985
Windrider	1986
The Time Guardian	1987
The Man from Snowy River II	1987

ESMA CANNON (1896-1972)

Tiny Australian character actress seen for many years in
spinsterish portrayals, often of the comedy variety.

The £5 Man	1937
The Last Adventurers	1937
Ladies in Love	1937
I See Ice	1938
It's in the Air	1938
Trouble Brewing	1939
I Met a Murderer	1939
The Spy in Black	1939
Poison Pen	1939
The Briggs Family	1940
Asking For Trouble	1941
Quiet Wedding	1941
The Big Blockade	1941
The Young Mr. Pitt	1942
It's In the Bag	1943
The Way Ahead	1944
English Without Tears	1944
Don't Take It to Heart	1944
A Canterbury Tale	1944
The Years Between	1946
Jassy	1947
Holiday Camp	1947

Here Come the Huggetts	1948
Vote for Huggett	1948
Marry Me	1949
Helter Skelter	1949
Fools Rush In	1949
The Huggetts Abroad	1949
Guilt Is My Shadow	1950
Last Holiday	1950
Double Confession	1950
Crow Hollow	1952
The Steel Key	1953
Noose for a Lady	1953
Trouble in Store	1953
The Case of Soho Red	1954
The Sleeping Tiger	1954
Out of the Clouds	1955
The Dam Busters	1955
Sailor Beware	1956
A Touch of the Sun	1956
Three Men in a Boat	1956
Further Up the Creek	1958
I'm All Right, Jack	1959
Jack the Ripper	1959
Expresso Bongo	1959
Inn for Trouble	1960
Carry On Constable	1960
The Flesh and the Fiends	1960
Doctor in Love	1960
No Kidding	1960
Carry on Regardless	1961
What a Carve Up!	1961
Over the Odds	1961
Raising the Wind	1961
In the Doghouse	1961
We Joined the Navy	1962
The Fast Lady	1962
On the Beat	1962
Carry On Cruising	1962
Nurse on Wheels	1963
Hide and Seek	1963
Carry On Cabby	1963

DIANE CILENTO (1933-   )

Attractive, adaptable Australian actress of stage (since 1949)
and films, also novelist. Formerly married to Sean Connery.

Wings of Danger	1952
Moulin Rouge	1953
All Hallowe'en	1953
Meet Mr. Lucifer	1953
The Passing Stranger	1954
The Angel Who Pawned Her Harp	1955
Passage Home	1955
A Woman for Joe	1955
The Small Servant	1955
The Taming of the Shrew	1956
The Admirable Crichton	1957
The Truth About Women	1958
Strange Interlude	1958
Jet Storm	1959
The Full Treatment	1961
The Naked Edge	1961
I Thank a Fool	1962
The Breaking Point	1962
Tom Jones	1963
The Third Secret	1964
Rattle of a Simple Man	1964
The Agony and the Ecstasy	1965
Hombre	1966
Once upon a Tractor	1967
You Only Live Twice	1967
Dial M for Murder	1967
Negatives	1968
Z.P.G.	1972
The Wicker Man	1973
Hitler: The Last Ten Days	1973
Spell of Evil	1973
Tiger Lily	1975
Partners	1981
For the Term of His Natural Life	1982
The Boy Who Had Everything	1984

TRILBY CLARK

Australian leading lady of stage and screen during the early
sound era; also in Hollywood.

The Lover of Camille	1924
Silent Sanderson	1925
Carry On	1927
Maria Marten	1928
The Passing of Mr. Quin	1928
Chick	1928
God's Clay	1929
The Compulsory Husband	1930
Harmony Heaven	1930
The Night Porter	1930
The Squeaker	1930
The Devil's Maze	1930

JOHN CLAYTON

Australian actor seen on television and in some motion pictures.

Sidecar Racers	1975
High Rolling	1977
Newsfront	1978
Dawn	1979
High Tide	1986
Warm Nights on a Slow Train	1987
Boundaries of the Heart	1987

CHARLES COLEMAN (1885-1951)

Australian supporting and character actor who appeared in numerous Hollywood motion pictures.

Big Dan	1923
Second Hand Love	1923
That French Lady	1924
The Vagabond Trail	1924
Sand	1926
Good Morning Judge	1928
That's My Daddy	1928
What a Man!	1929
Lawful Larceny	1930
Once a Gentleman	1930
Beyond Victory	1931
Bachelor Apartment	1931
The Heart of New York	1932

Play Girl	1932
Merrily We Go to Hell	1932
Winner Take All	1932
Jewel Robbery	1932
Diplomaniacs	1933
Midnight Club	1933
Gallant Lady	1933
Sailor Be Good	1933
The Gay Divorcee	1934
Embarrassing Moments	1934
Born to Be Bad	1934
The Merry Finks	1934
Housewife	1934
Million Dollar Ransom	1934
Down to Their Last Yacht	1934
Becky Sharp	1935
The Goose and the Gander	1935
His Family Tree	1935
Magnificent Obsession	1935
Gold Diggers of 1935	1935
Fury	1936
Born to Dance	1936
Colleen	1936
Her Master's Voice	1936
Don't Get Personal	1936
Everybody's Old Man	1936
Poor Little Rich Girl	1936
Mummy's Boys	1936
Walking on Air	1936
Lloyds of London	1936
Love Is News	1937
Too Many Wives	1937
There Goes My Girl	1937
Fight for Your Lady	1937
Three Smart Girls	1937
The Go-Getter	1937
Captains Courageous	1937
Shall We Dance	1937
100 Men and a Girl	1937
Alexander's Ragtime Band	1938
Penrod & His Twin Brother	1938
Little Miss Broadway	1938
Gateway	1938
The Rage of Paris	1938
That Certain Age	1938

Little Orphan Annie	1938
Mexican Spitfire	1939
You Can't Cheat an Honest Man	1939
First Love	1939
Raffles	1939
In Name Only	1939
The Westerner	1940
Mexican Spitfire Out West	1940
Buck Privates	1941
Free and Easy	1941
It Started with Eve	1941
Maisie Was a Lady	1941
Lady in a Jam	1942
Twin Beds	1942
Almost Married	1942
Miss Annie Rooney	1942
Between Us Girls	1942
Highways by Nights	1942
Arabian Nights	1942
Design for Scandal	1942
Air Raid Wardens	1943
It Ain't Hay	1943
It Comes Up Love	1943
Pittsburgh	1943
She's for Me	1943
Girl Crazy	1943
Lady in the Dark	1944
Mrs. Parkington	1944
Once upon a Time	1944
Frenchman's Creek	1944
In Society	1944
The Whistler	1944
The Picture of Dorian Gray	1945
Missing Corpse	1945
The Stork Club	1945
Diamond Horseshoe	1945
Kitty	1945
Earl Carrol's Vanities	1945
Anchors Aweigh	1945
Monsieur Beaucaire	1946
Cluny Brown	1946
In High Gear	1946
Oh Professor Behave	1946
Magnificent Rogue	1946
The Runaround	1946

Never Say Goodbye	1946
Ziegfeld Follies	1946
Pilgrim Lady	1947
The Imperfect Lady	1947
Ladie's Man	1947
Lured	1947
Variety Girl	1947
Love from a Stranger	1947
Trouble Makers	1948
My Friend Irma	1949
Oil's Well That Ends Well	1949
Texas Tough Guy	1950

CLYDE COOK (1892-1984)

Australian character actor long in Hollywood with music hall experience as well from 1908. Former dancer and acrobat.

The Eskimo	1922
He Who Gets Slapped	1924
So This Is Marriage	1925
The Winning of Barbara Worth	1926
White Gold	1927
The Climbers	1927
Barbed Wire	1927
Good Time Charley	1927
The Brute	1927
Miss Nobody	1928
Pay as You Enter	1928
Docks of New York	1928
Beware of Married Men	1928
Captain Lash	1929
Dangerous Woman	1929
The Spieler	1929
Strong Boy	1929
Lucky in Love	1929
The Taming of the Shrew	1929
Jazz Heaven	1929
Officer O'Brien	1930
Women Everywhere	1930
Sunny	1930
The Dawn Patrol	1930
Daybreak	1931
Never the Twain Shall Meet	1931

The Secret Witness	1931
Blondie of the Follies	1932
Oliver Twist	1933
West of Singapore	1933
The Barbary Coast	1935
White Angel	1936
Wee Willie Winkie	1937
Love Under Fire	1937
Kidnapped	1938
Storm Over Bengal	1938
Arrest Bulldog Drummond	1939
Bulldog Drummond's Secret Police	1939
The Light That Failed	1939
The Little Princess	1939
The Sea Hawk	1940
Ladies in Retirement	1941
White Cargo	1942
Mysterious Doctor	1943
Forever and a Day	1943
The Man from Down Under	1943
Follow the Boys	1944
To Each His Own	1946
The Verdict	1946
Donovan's Reef	1963

TERENCE COOPER

Australian leading man and latterly supporting player of screen and TV.

No Safety Ahead	1958
Top Floor Girl	1959
Walk a Tightrope	1963
Calculated Risk	1963
Man in the Middle	1964
Casino Royale	1967
Beyond Reasonable Doubt	1980
Heart of the Stag	1983
Sylvia	1985
Defence Play	1987
Infidelity	1987
No Way Out	1987

DAME CICELY COURTNEIDGE (1893-1980)

Distinguished, vivacious Australian comedienne and entertainer
of stage (from 1901) and screen; reveled in eccentricity. Long
married to Jack Hulbert, with whom she frequently appeared.
Autobiography: Cicely, 1953.

British Screen Tatler No. 10	1928
Elstree Calling	1930
The Ghost Train	1931
Jack's the Boy	1932
Happy Ever After	1932
Soldiers of the King	1933
Falling for You	1933
Night and Day	1933
Aunt Sally	1934
A Woman in Command	1934
Things Are Looking Up	1935
Me and Marlborough	1935
The Perfect Gentleman	1935
Everybody Dance	1936
Take My Tip	1937
The Imperfect Lady	1937
Under Your Hat	1940
Spider's Web	1960
The L-Shaped Room	1962
Ninety Years On	1964
Those Magnificent Men in Their Flying Machines	1965
The Wrong Box	1966
Not Now Darling	1973

RUTH CRACKNELL

Australian character actress mainly on stage and TV; films
rare.

Smiley Gets a Gun	1958
Night of the Prowler	1979
The Chant of Jimmie Blacksmith	1980
The Best of Friends	1982
Mother and Son	1986

MARSHAL CROSBY (1883-1954)

Australian character player seen in a few films down under.

The Overlanders	1946
Pacific Adventure	1947
Eureka Stockade	1949
Kangaroo	1952

MAX CULLEN

Australian leading man and supporting actor of films and television.

The Office Picnic	1974
Summerfield	1977
Sunday Too Far Away	1977
Blue Fin	1978
Dimboola	1979
The Odd Angry Shot	1979
Sam	1980
My Brilliant Career	1980
Hard Knocks	1981
Running On Empty	1982
Midnite Spares	1982
Freedom	1983
Starstruck	1983
The Return of Captain Invincible	1983
Times Are Changing	1984
Stanley	1984
The Last Bastion	1984
The Cowra Breakout	1985
The Flying Doctors	1986
Sons of Cain	1987
Boundaries of the Heart	1987

ALLAN CUTHBERTSON (1920-88)

Australian actor, long in Britain, frequently seen in unsympathetic, weakling, or slightly haughty roles. Also much on television. Also a good light comedian on occasion.

Carrington VC	1954

Portrait of Alison	1955
The Man Who Never Was	1956
Eyewitness	1956
On Such a Night	1956
Doublecross	1956
Dick Turpin-Highwayman	1956
Cloak Without Dagger	1956
Anastasia	1956
Sword of Truth	1956
Point of Crisis	1956
Yangtse Incident	1956
The Suspects	1957
Barnacle Bill	1957
The Passionate Stranger	1957
Law and Disorder	1958
Ice Cold in Alex	1958
I Was Monty's Double	1958
The Crowning Touch	1959
Stranglers of Bombay	1959
Room at the Top	1959
Killers of Kilimanjaro	1959
Shake Hands with the Devil	1959
The Devil's Disciple	1959
Tunes of Glory	1960
Survival	1960
The Guns of Navarone	1961
On the Double	1961
The Malpas Mystery	1961
Man at the Carlton Tower	1961
Burnt Offering	1962
Freud	1962
The Boys	1962
Solo for Sparrow	1962
The Fast Lady	1962
Term of Trial	1962
Vengeance	1962
Tamahine	1963
The Informers	1963
Bitter Harvest	1963
Mouse on the Moon	1963
The Running Man	1963
Nine Hours to Rama	1963
The Seventh Dawn	1964
Life at the Top	1965
Operation Crossbow	1965

Game for Three Losers	1965
Cast a Giant Shadow	1965
Reign of Terror	1965
The Bruce-Partington Plans	1966
Press for Time	1966
Half a Sixpence	1967
Rocket to the Moon	1967
The Trygon Factor	1967
Thin Air	1968
Sinful Davy	1969
The Body Stealers	1969
Captain Nemo & the Underwater City	1969
The Firechasers	1970
One More Time	1970
Performance	1970
The Adventurers	1970
Assault	1971
Diamonds on Wheels	1972
In the Devil's Garden	1974
The Chiffy Kids	1976
Terry and June	1979
The Outsider	1980
Hopscotch	1980
The Mirror Crack'd	1980
The Sea Wolves	1980
Shelley	1981
The Winds of War	1982
Invitation to the Wedding	1983
13 at Dinner	1985
Edge of Darkness	1986
Still Crazy Like a Fox	1987

JUDY DAVIS (1955-)

Australian leading lady of films and television of the eighties.

High Rolling	1977
My Brilliant Career	1979
Water Under the Bridge	1980
Hoodwink	1981
Heatwave	1981
A Woman Called Golda	1982
The Winter of Our Dreams	1982
The Merry Wives of Windsor	1983

Who Dares Wins	1983
A Passage to India	1984
Kangaroo	1985
Clean Straw for Nothing	1986
Rocket to the Moon	1986
High Tide	1987

ED DEVEREAUX

Australian supporting performer of films and television, often in comedy parts; also the star of TV series Skippy. (1969).

Carry on Sergeant	1958
Carry On Nurse	1959
The Savage Innocents	1959
The Captain's Table	1959
There Was a Crooked Man	1960
Man in the Moon	1961
Carry On Regardless	1961
Carry On Cruising	1962
The Wrong Arm of the Law	1962
The Password Is Courage	1962
Very Important Person	1962
Mix Me a Person	1962
Ladies Who Do	1963
Never Put It in Writing	1963
Carry On Jack	1963
Live It Up	1963
They're a Weird Mob	1966
Journey Out of Darkness	1967
The Nickel Queen	1971
Bless This House	1973
The Death of Adolf Hitler	1974
Barry Mackenzie Holds His Own	1974
Come Back Little Sheba	1976
Pressure	1977
Money Movers	1978
Edward and Mrs. Simpson	1978
The Intruders	1979
Kings	1983
The Dismissal	1983
Robbery Under Arms	1984
Reunion at Fairborough	1985
Dinner Date	1985
Bon Voyage	1987

ARTHUR DIGNAM

Australian actor of stage, motion pictures, and television.

The Priest	1972
Summer of Secrets	1975
Between the Wars	1975
Jock Petersen	1975
Libido	1976
The Devil's Payground	1977
Cathy's Child	1979
The Chant of Jimmie Blacksmith	1980
Grendel Grendel Grendel	1982
Dead Kids	1982
We of the Never Never	1982
The Dismissal	1983
The Return of Captain Invincible	1983
The Wild Duck	1983
The Schippan Mystery	1984
The Right Hand Man	1985
Burke and Wills	1985
Comrades	1986
The Everlasting Secret Family	1987
Those Dear Departed	1987

GUY DOLEMAN (1923-)

Australian actor of films and TV who mainly plays unruffled or no-nonsense characters. Also in Hollywood.

Kangaroo	1952
Phantom Stockade	1953
His Majesty O'Keefe	1954
Dial M For Murder	1954
Smiley	1956
The Shiralee	1957
Smiley Gets a Gun	1958
On the Beach	1958
Captain Sinbad	1963
The Partner	1963
The System	1964
Boy with a Flute	1964
Thunderball	1965
The Ipcress File	1965

The Idol	1966
Funeral in Berlin	1966
Twist of Sand	1967
Billion Dollar Brain	1967
The Deadly Bees	1967
A Dangerous Summer	1982
Early Frost	1982
Goodbye Paradise	1983
Hell Raiders	1987

TERENCE DONOVAN

Australian actor who's been seen in occasional motion pictures.

Money Movers	1978
The Getting of Wisdom	1979
Breaker Morant	1980
The Man from Snowy River	1982
The Winds of Jarrah	1983
Night of Shadows	1984
Fortress	1985
Death of a Soldier	1986
Emma's War	1986
Room to Move	1987

DAVID DUNBAR (1893-1953)

Australian actor primarily in Hollywood, popular during the twenties.

Trail Dust	1924
The 40th Door	1924
Leather Stockings	1924
North of 36	1924
The Bloodhound	1925
Fair Play	1925
The Cowboy Musketeer	1925
Riding the Wind	1925
Galloping Vengeance	1925
Man of Nerve	1925
Galloping Cowboy	1926
Non-Stop Flight	1926
Beyond the Rockies	1926

King of Kings	1927
The Boy Rider	1927
Bronco Buster	1927
Gold From Weepah	1927
Arizona Whirlwind	1928
Fighting Hombre	1928
Plunging Hoofs	1929
The Streets of London	1929
The Second Mate	1929
Human Cargo	1929
Three Men in a Cart	1929
Downstream	1929
The Return of Dr. Fu Manchu	1930
The Great Impersonation	1935
Kidnapped	1938
Mrs. Miniver	1942
If Winter Comes	1947
Summer Holiday	1948
Young Man with a Horn	1950

LEON ERROL (1881-1951)

Bald-headed Australian comedy character star, long in Hollywood where he specialized in playing drunken, henpecked, flustered, or nervous characters.

Yolanda	1924
Clothes Make the Pirate	1925
Sally	1925
Lunatic at Large	1927
One Heavenly Night	1929
Let's Merge	1930
Paramount on Parade	1930
Only Saps Work	1930
Queen of Scandal	1930
Finn and Hattie	1931
Her Majesty, Love	1931
Practice Shots	1932
Alice in Wonderland	1933
Three Little Swigs	1933
The Poor Fish	1933
Hold Your Temper	1933
We're Not Dressing	1934
The Notorious Sophie Lang	1934

The Captain Hates the Sea	1934
Autobiography	1934
No More Bridge	1934
Perfectly Mismated	1934
Good Morning, Eve	1934
Service with a Smile	1934
Fixing a Stew	1934
One Too Many	1934
Counselitis	1935
Honeymoon Bridge	1935
Home Work	1935
Salesmanship Ahoy	1935
Hit and Run	1935
Princess O'Hara	1935
Coronado	1935
Down the Ribber	1936
Pirate Party on Catalina Isle	1936
Wholesailing Along	1936
One Live Ghost	1936
Make a Wish	1937
Wrong Romance	1937
Should Wives Work?	1937
Dummy Owner	1937
Rented Riot	1937
His Pest Friend	1938
Stage Fright	1938
The Jitters	1938
Major Difficulties	1938
Crime Rave	1938
Birth Quakes	1938
The Girl from Mexico	1939
Career	1939
Dancing Co-Ed	1939
Mexican Spitfire	1939
Home Boner	1939
Moving Vanities	1939
Ring Madness	1939
Wrong Room	1939
Truth Aches	1939
Scrappily Married	1939
He Asked for It	1940
Bested by a Beard	1940
Tattled Television	1940
The Fired Man	1940
Pop Always Pays	1940

Mexican Spitfire Out West	1940
The Golden Fleecing	1940
Six Lessons from Madame la Zonga	1941
Where Did You Get That Girl?	1941
Hurry Charley, Hurry	1941
Mexican Spitfire's Baby	1941
Melody Lane	1941
Moonlight in Hawaii	1941
Never Give a Sucker an Even Break	1941
When Wifeie's Away	1941
Polo Phony	1941
Panic in the Parlor	1941
The Man I Cured	1941
Who's a Dummy?	1941
Homework	1941
Mexican Spitfire at Sea	1942
Mexican Spitfire Sees a Ghost	1942
Mexican Spitfire's Elephant	1942
Wedded Blitz	1942
Framing Father	1942
Mail Trouble	1942
Dear! Dear!	1942
Pretty Dolly	1942
Double Up	1943
Family Feud	1943
Gem Jams	1943
Radio Runaround	1943
Seeing Nellie Home	1943
Cutie on Duty	1943
Wedtime Stories	1943
Cowboy in Manhattan	1943
Strictly in the Groove	1943
Mexican Spitfire's Blessed Event	1943
Follow the Band	1943
Higher and Higher	1943
Gals Inc.	1943
Hat Check Honey	1944
The Invisible Man's Revenge	1944
Slightly Terrific	1944
Twilight on the Prairie	1944
Babes on Swing Street	1944
Say Uncle	1944
Poppa Knows Worst	1944
Price Unlimited	1944
Girls Girls Girls	1944
Triple Trouble	1944

He Forgot to Remember	1944
She Gets Her Man	1945
What a Blonde!	1945
Under Western Skies	1945
Mama Loves Papa	1945
Let's Go Stepping	1945
Birthday Blues	1945
It Shouldn't Happen to a Dog	1945
Double Honeymoon	1945
Beware of Redheads	1946
Oh Professor, Behave	1946
Maid Trouble	1946
Twin Husbands	1946
I'll Take Milk	1946
Follow That Blonde	1946
Joe Palooka Champ	1946
Gentleman Joe Palooka	1946
Joe Palooka in the Knockout	1947
Borrowed Blonde	1947
Wife Tames Wolf	1947
In Room 303	1947
Hired Husband	1947
Blondes Away	1947
The Spook Speaks	1947
Joe Palooka in Fighting Mad	1948
The Noose Hangs High	1948
Joe Palooka in Winner Take All	1948
Variety Time	1948
Bet Your Life	1948
Don't Fool Your Wife	1948
Secretary Trouble	1948
Bachelor Blues	1948
Uninvited Blonde	1948
Backstage Follies	1948
Joe Palooka in the Big Fight	1949
Joe Palooka in Counterpunch	1949
Joe Palooka Meets Humphrey	1949
Dad Always Pays	1949
Cactus Cut-Up	1949
I Can't Remember	1949
Oil's Well That Ends Well	1949
Sweet Cheat	1949
Shocking Affair	1949
High and Dizzy	1950
Joe Palooka in Humphrey Takes a Chance	1950

Texas Tough Guy	1950
Spooky Wooky	1950
Chinatown Chump	1951
Punchy Pancho	1951
One Wild Night	1951
Deal Me In	1951
Too Many Wives	1951
Footlight Varieties	1951
Lord Epping Returns	1951

FREDERICK ESMELTON (1872-1933)

Australian supporting actor of stage and screen in Hollywood, also director.

The Avalanche	1919
Can a Woman Love Twice?	1923
Three Wise Fools	1923
Boston Blackie	1923
The Custard Cup	1923
Dulcy	1923
The Darling of New York	1923
The Rustle of Silk	1923
Conductor 1492	1924
Lady of the Night	1925
Smooth as Satin	1925
Red Hot Tires	1925
Raffles	1925
California Straight Ahead	1926
Kid Boots	1926
Shield of Honour	1927
The Gay Defender	1927
Romance of a Rogue	1928
The Baby Cyclone	1928
The Chinese Parrot	1928
Two Lovers	1929
The Michigan Kid	1929
Born to Love	1931

JOHN EWART

Australian supporting and sometimes leading man of films and TV.

Angel Gear	1976
Let the Balloon Go	1976
The Love Epidemic	1976
Sunday Too Far Away	1977
Newsfront	1978
Picture Show Man	1978
Blue Fire Lady	1979
Deadline	1981
Save the Lady	1981
Wal to Wall	1982
Kitty and the Bagman	1983
Crosstalk	1983
Razorback	1983
Bush Christmas	1984
Kindred Spirits	1984
Supersleuth	1984
A Slice of Life	1985
Frog Dreaming	1985
The Big Hurt	1986
The Last Frontier	1986
Arthur & the Square Knight of the Round Table	1987
Dear Cardholder	1987
Colour in the Creek	1987

TRADER FAULKNER (1930-)

Australian supporting actor of stage who has appeared in occasional films. Also author.

Mr. Denning Drives North	1951
A Killer Walks	1952
24 Hours in a Woman's Life	1952
A Question of Adultery	1958
Macbeth	1960
The Spanish Sword	1962
The Bay of St. Michel	1963
The Murder Game	1965
A High Wind in Jamaica	1965
Life at Stake	1977
The Faraday Kidnap	1977
Eyeless in Gaza	1981
The House in Paris	1982
Sword of Honour	1984

Duty Free	1985
Call Me Mister	1986

JOHN FERNSIDE

Australian actor who was seen in a few films during the forties.

The Overlanders	1946
Bush Christmas	1947
Eureka Stockade	1948

NOEL FERRIER

Australian supporting performer of television and some films.
Also author, producer, and radio personality.

Demonstrator	1971
Alvin Purple	1973
Alvin Rides Again	1974
Avengers of the Reef	1974
Scobie Malone	1975
Eliza Fraser	1976
No Room to Run	1977
Deathcheaters	1978
Turkey Shoot	1982
The Return of Captain Invincible	1983
Great Expectations	1987
Vietnam	1987

LEWIS FIANDER (1938-   )

Australian supporting and occasional leading man of stage,
television and screen.

The Password Is Courage	1962
The VIPs	1963
I Start Counting	1969
Sweeney Todd	1970
Dr. Jekyll and Sister Hyde	1971
Dr. Phibes Rises Again	1972
The Abdication	1974
Death Is Child's Play	1975

Notorious Woman	1975
Not Now Comrade	1976
Who Can Kill a Child?	1977
Sweeney II	1978
Island of the Damned	1978
Pride and Prejudice	1979
The Case of the Discontented Soldier	1982
The Late Nancy Irving	1984
The Doctor and the Devils	1985
Lytton's Diary	1985
On Wings of Fire	1986
The Two Mrs. Grenvilles	1987

PETER FINCH (1916-1977)

Outstanding, intelligent star of stage (from 1934) and screen, latterly in international films. Also at one time a leading radio performer (in Australia).

Magic Shoes	1935
Dad and Dave Come to Town	1937
Red Sky at Morning	1937
Mr. Chedworth Steps Out	1938
Ants in His Pants	1939
Another Threshold	1942
While There's Still Time	1942
South-West Pacific	1943
The Rats of Tobruk	1944
Jungle Patrol (voice)	1944
Indonesia Calling (voice)	1945
The Power and the Glory	1945
A Son Is Born	1946
Native Earth (voice)	1946
The Nomads (voice)	1947
The Hunt (voice)	1948
Eureka Stockade	1948
The Corroboree (voice)	1949
Train of Events	1949
The Wooden Horse	1950
The Miniver Story	1950
Robin Hood	1952
Gilbert and Sullivan	1953
The Heart of the Matter	1953
Father Brown	1954

Elephant Walk	1954
Make Me an Offer	1955
The Dark Avenger	1955
Passage Home	1955
Simon and Laura	1955
Josephine and Men	1955
The Queen in Australia (voice)	1956
Melbourne-Olympic City (voice)	1956
The Royal Tour of New South Wales (voice)	1956
Battle of the River Plate	1956
A Town Like Alice	1956
The Shiralee	1957
Robbery Under Arms	1957
Windom's Way	1957
Operation Amsterdam	1958
A Far Cry	1958
The Nun's Story	1959
Kidnapped	1959
The Trials of Oscar Wilde	1960
The Sins of Rachel Cade	1960
The Breaking Point	1961
No Love for Johnnie	1961
The Day	1961
I Thank a Fool	1962
In the Cool of the Day	1963
The Girl with Green Eyes	1964
First Men in the Moon	1964
The Pumpkin Eater	1964
Come Spy with Me	1965
Judith	1965
The Flight of the Phoenix	1965
10:30 PM Summer	1966
Far from the Madding Crowd	1967
The Legend of Lylah Clare	1968
The Greatest Mother of Them All	1969
The Red Tent	1971
Sunday Bloody Sunday	1971
Something of Hide	1971
England Made Me	1972
Lost Horizon	1973
A Bequest to the Nation	1973
The Abdication	1974
Network	1976
Raid on Entebbe	1977
A Look at Liv	1978

JOHN FINLAYSON

Australian supporting actor, mainly on TV, who has been seen in a few films.

Alvin Purple	1973
Alvin Rides Again	1974
Lonely Hearts	1983
My First Wife	1985

LEWIS FITZ-GERALD

Australian leading actor of the eighties, also on TV.

Breaker Morant	1980
We of the Never Never	1982
Fighting Back	1983
The Boy Who Had Everything	1984
Times Raging	1985
The More Things Change	1986
The Flying Doctors	1986
Warm Nights on a Slow Train	1987

CLAUDE FLEMING (1884-1952)

Australian writer, producer, director, and occasional actor in Hollywood.

The Sword of Damocles	1920
Unholy Night	1929
Mamba	1930
Captain of the Guard	1930
Bride of the Regiment	1930
One Night at Susie's	1930

IAN FLEMING (1888-1969)

Australian character star of stage (from 1904) and films who was often cast as a professional man, also well-remembered as Dr. Watson to Arthur Wontner's Sherlock Holmes during the 1930s. No relation to writer Ian Fleming (1906-1964), creator of James Bond.

Second to None	1926
The Ware Case	1928
The Devil's Maze	1929
School for Scandal	1930
The Sleeping Cardinal	1931
The Missing Rembrandt	1932
After Dark	1932
Lucky Girl	1932
Called Back	1933
Paris Plane	1933
Passing Shadows	1934
The Third Clue	1934
Riverside Murder	1935
School for Stars	1935
Sexton Blake & the Mademoiselle	1935
The Crouching Beast	1935
The Triumph of Sherlock Holmes	1935
21 Today	1936
Prison Breaker	1936
Royal Eagle	1936
Hearts of Humanity	1936
Darby and Joan	1937
Racing Romance	1937
Jump for Glory	1937
Silver Blaze	1937
The Claydon Treasure Mystery	1938
The Return of Carol Deane	1938
Almost a Honeymoon	1938
Ghost Tales Retold	1938
Dial 999	1938
The Reverse Be My Lot	1938
Quiet Please	1938
Double or Quits	1938
If I Were Boss	1938
Bad Boy	1938
Dead Men Are Dangerous	1939
Men Without Honour	1939
The Lion Has Wings	1939
The Nursemaid Who Disappeared	1939
Shadowed Eyes	1939
Me and My Pal	1939
Night Train to Munich	1940
Branded	1940
The Good Old Days	1940

Tilly of Bloomsbury	1940
The Briggs Family	1940
Three Silent Men	1940
Gentleman of Venture	1940
Jeannie	1941
Hatter's Castle	1941
Ships with Wings	1941
Sabotage at Sea	1942
Let the People Sing	1942
Salute John Citizen	1942
They Flew Alone	1942
Talk About Jacqueline	1942
Soldiers Without Uniform	1942
They Met in the Dark	1943
Bell Bottom George	1943
The Yellow Canary	1943
Up With the Lark	1943
The Butler's Dilemma	1943
Tawny Pipit	1944
He Snoops to Conquer	1944
They Knew Mr. Knight	1945
I Didn't Do It	1945
George in Civvy Street	1946
Appointment with Crime	1946
Captain Boycott	1947
Quartet	1948
A Matter of Murder	1949
For Them That Trespass	1949
What a Carry On	1949
School for Randle	1949
Shadow of the Past	1950
The Woman in Question	1950
Chelsea Story	1951
Salute the Toff	1952
Crow Hollow	1952
The Voice of Merrill	1952
Hammer the Toff	1952
Circumstantial Evidence	1952
Come Back Peter	1952
Murder Will Out	1953
Recoil	1953
It's a Grand Life	1953
Park Plaza 605	1953
Deadly Nightshade	1953
The Saint's Return	1953

Stryker of the Yard	1953
Companions in Crime	1954
The Seekers	1954
Delayed Action	1954
The Embezzler	1954
Police Dog	1955
Guilty	1956
High Flight	1957
A Woman Possessed	1958
Innocent Meeting	1959
Web of Suspicion	1959
Man Accused	1959
Crash Drive	1959
Make Mine Mink	1960
Your Money or Your Wife	1960
The Trials of Oscar Wilde	1960
The Flesh and the Fiends	1960
Too Hot to Handle	1960
Bluebeard's Ten Honeymoons	1960
No My Darling Daughter	1961
The Boys	1962
Return of a Stranger	1962
The Lamp in Assassin Mews	1962
What Every Woman Wants	1962
Tamahine	1963
Crooks in Cloisters	1963
70 Deadly Pills	1964
The Return of Mr. Moto	1965
River Rivals	1966
The Forsyte Saga	1967

ERROL FLYNN (1909-1959)

Swashbuckling Australian leading man, primarily seen in Hollywood. Noted for being just as much a rogue off screen as on. Former shipping clerk and sailor.

Dr. H. Erben's New Guinea Expedition	1932
In the Wake of the Bounty	1933
Murder at Monte Carlo	1934
Case of the Curious Bride	1934
Don't Bet on Blondes	1935
Captain Blood	1935
Pirate Party on Catalina Isle	1936

Charge of the Light Brigade	1936
The Green Light	1936
Another Dawn	1937
The Perfect Specimen	1937
The Prince and the Pauper	1937
Four's a Crowd	1938
The Adventures of Robin Hood	1938
The Sisters	1938
The Dawn Patrol	1938
Dodge City	1939
Virginia City	1939
Elizabeth the Queen	1939
The Sea Hawk	1940
Santa Fe Trail	1940
Footsteps in the Dark	1941
Dive Bomber	1941
They Died with Their Boots On	1941
Gentleman Jim	1942
Desperate Journey	1942
Edge of Darkness	1943
Northern Pursuit	1943
Thank Your Lucky Stars	1943
Uncertain Glory	1944
Objective Burma	1945
San Antonio	1945
Never Say Goodbye	1945
Cry Wolf	1946
Escape Me Never	1947
Silver River	1947
New Adventures of Don Juan	1948
That Forsyte Woman	1949
It's a Great Feeling	1949
Hello God	1950
Montana	1950
Rocky Mountain	1950
Kim	1951
Adventures of Captain Fabian	1951
Mara Maru	1952
Against All Flags	1952
Cruise of the Zaca	1952
Deep Sea Fishing	1952
William Tell	1953
The Master of Ballantrae	1953
Crossed Swords	1954
Lilacs in the Spring	1955

The Dark Avenger	1955
King's Rhapsody	1955
The Big Blockade	1956
The Sword of Vallon	1956
Istanbul	1957
The Sun Also Rises	1957
Without Incident	1957
The 100th Night of Don Juan	1957
Rescued	1957
The Duel	1957
Too Much Too Soon	1958
The Roots of Heaven	1958
Cuban Rebel Girls	1959
The Golden Shanty	1959

MOYRA FRASER (1923-)

Australian comedy actress, seen sporadically in films. Also
on TV, latterly in series Danger UXB (1980).

Madeleine	1950
The Dancing Years	1950
The Man Who Loved Redheads	1955
Left, Right and Centre	1959
The VIPs	1963
Here We Go Round the Mulberry Bush	1967
Prudence and the Pill	1968
The Boy Friend	1971
Danger UXB	1980

WILLIAM FRESHMAN (1905-)

Australian leading man and screenwriter; former property
boy (1918).

First Men in the Moon	1919
Fifth Form at St. Dominic's	1921
Leaves From My Life	1921
The Lights O' London	1922
Creation	1922
Faust	1922
Was She Guilty?	1922
Hims Ancient and Modern	1922
The Sporting Twelve	1922

Luck of the Navy	1927
The Guns of Loos	1928
Glamorous Youth	1928
The Rising Generation	1928
Widecombe Fair	1928
Broken Romance	1929
Those Who Love	1929
Greek Street	1930
Star Impersonations	1930
Thread O'Scarlet	1930
Night Shadows	1931
Bachelor's Baby	1932
F.P.1.	1933
Love's Old Sweet Song	1933
Lucky Blaze	1933
The Scarlet Pimpernel	1935
Limelight	1936
The Man at the Gate	1941

COLIN FRIELS

Australian leading man of the eighties, also on television.

Monkey Grip	1983
Buddies	1984
Prisoners	1985
Coolangatta Gold	1985
Kangaroo	1986
High Tide	1987
Warm Nights on a Slow Train	1987
Ground Zero	1987
Bodily Harm	1987

SHAYLE GARDNER (1890-1955)

New Zealand character actor of stage (from 1913) and screen; former architect. Also in Hollywood.

Comin' Thro' the Rye	1922
Poetic License	1922
St. Elmo	1923
The Wandering Jew	1923
Indian Love Lyrics	1923
Guy Fawkes	1923

Sailors Don't Care	1928
Tommy Atkins	1928
The Three Passions	1928
The Alley Cat	1929
Disraeli	1929
Three Live Ghosts	1929
New Adventures of Dr. Fu Manchu	1930
The Return of Dr. Fu Manchu	1931
Lloyd of the C.I.D.	1931
The Lodger	1932
Diamond Cut Diamond	1932
The River House Ghost	1932
The Medium	1934
Sabotage	1934
The Love Test	1935
Her Last Affaire	1935
The Brown Wallet	1936
Wolf's Clothing	1936
The Scat Burglars	1937
Under the Red Robe	1937
Discoveries	1939

MEL GIBSON (1951-)

Australian leading actor of the 1980s, also in international films.

Summer City	1979
Mad Max	1979
The Sullivans	1979
Tickled Pink	1980
Tim	1980
The Z Men	1981
Gallipoli	1981
Mad Max II	1982
The Hero	1982
The Year of Living Dangerously	1982
Running Man	1983
The River	1984
The Bounty	1984
Mrs. Soffel	1984
Burton and Speke	1985
Mad Max III	1985
Clean Straw for Nothing	1986
Lethal Weapon	1987

Return to the Bridge on the River
    Kwai   1987
Tetley   1987
Tequila Sunrise   1987

IAN GILMOUR

Supporting and sometimes leading Australian actor of motion
pictures and television.

Mouth to Mouth	1978
The Odd Angry Shot	1979
Just Out of Reach	1979
The Chant of Jimmie Blacksmith	1980
A Burning Man	1981
A Dangerous Summer	1982
Going Down	1983
The Coca Cola Kid	1984
Room to Move	1987

ROBERT GREIG (1879-1958)

Portly Australian character star of the 1930s and 1940s in
Hollywood; generally seen in pompous or supercilious roles.

Animal Crackers	1930
Paramount on Parade	1930
Tonight or Never	1931
Trouble in Paradise	1932
Jitters the Butler	1932
Stepping Sisters	1932
Beauty and the Boss	1932
Man Wanted	1932
The Cohens & Kellys in Hollywood	1932
The Tenderfoot	1932
Merrily We Go to Hell	1932
Jewel Robbery	1932
Horse Feathers	1932
Love Me Tonight	1932
Pleasure Cruise	1933
It's Great to Be Alive	1933
Peg O' My Heart	1933
They Just Had to Get Married	1933

Dangerously Yours	1933
Men Must Fight	1933
The Mind Reeder	1933
Easy to Love	1934
Upperworld	1934
One More River	1934
The Love Captive	1934
Cockeyed Cavaliers	1934
Clive of India	1935
Follies Bergere	1935
Woman Wanted	1935
The Bishop Misbehaves	1935
The Gay Deception	1935
I Live for Love	1935
Three Live Ghosts	1936
Rose Marie	1936
Unguarded Hour	1936
Small Town Girl	1936
Trouble for Two	1936
The Devil Doll	1936
Witch of Timbuktu	1936
The Suicide Club	1936
Right in Your Lap	1936
Theodora Goes Wild	1936
Lloyds of London	1936
Stowaway	1936
Easy to Take	1936
Michael O'Halloran	1936
Easy Living	1937
My Dead Miss Aldrich	1937
Lady Behave	1938
Midnight Intruder	1938
Adventures of Marco Polo	1938
Algiers	1938
Drums Along the Mowhawk	1939
Way Down South	1939
It Could Happen to You	1939
Hudson's Bay	1940
No Time for Comedy	1940
The Lady Eve	1941
Moon Over Miami	1941
Sullivan's Travels	1941
The Moon and Sixpence	1942
I Married a Witch	1942
Palm Beach Story	1943

The Great Moment	1944
Summer Storm	1944
Hollywood & Vine	1945
The Cheaters	1945
Earl Carroll's Vanities	1945
Nob Hill	1945
The Picture of Dorian Gray	1945
Love, Honor and Goodbye	1945
Unfaithfully Yours	1948
Bride of Vengeance	1949

ROBERT GRUBB

Australian leading and strong supporting actor of films of the eighties.

My Brilliant Career	1980
Gallipoli	1981
Phar Lap	1983
Robbery Under Arms	1984
Remember Me	1985
Mad Max III	1985
The Flying Doctors	1987

DAVID GULPILIL

Australian Aborigine actor in occasional supporting roles.

Walkabout	1971
Mad Dog Morgan	1976
Storm Boy	1977
The Last Wave	1978
Bill West	1982
The Right Stuff	1983
Crocodile Dundee	1986

JOHN HARGREAVES

Australian leading actor of motion pictures and television.

| Mad Dog Morgan | 1976 |
| The Removalists | 1976 |

Don's Party	1976
Eliza Fraser	1976
Deathcheaters	1978
The Odd Angry Shot	1979
Long Weekend	1980
Little Boy Lost	1980
Hoodwink	1981
Beyond Reasonable Doubt	1981
The Killing of Angel Street	1982
Careful He Might Hear You	1983
My First Wife	1984
Malcolm	1985
Comrades	1986
Sky Pirates	1986
Double Skulls	1986
The Bee-Eater	1986
The Place at the Coast	1987
Asking for Trouble	1987
The Alien Years	1987
Boundaries of the Heart	1987

LISA HARROW (1943-)

New Zealand leading actress seen much on television; occasional motion pictures. Married to Sam Neill.

The Devil Is a Woman	1975
All Creatures Great and Small	1975
Star Maidens	1976
1900	1977
It Souldn't Happen to a Vet	1978
Dr. Jekyll and Mr. Hyde	1981
The Final Conflict	1981
From a Far Country	1981
The Waterfall	1981
Nancy Astor	1982
Man and Superman	1983
Under Capricorn	1983
Other Halves	1984
Shaker Runn	1985
Lizzie's Pictures	1987
Always Afternoon	1987

CHRIS HAYWOOD

Australian actor, sometimes leading man of stage, screen, and
TV.

The Cars That Ate Paris	1975
The Great McCarthy	1976
The Removalists	1976
The Trespassers	1976
In Search of Anna	1977
Deathcheaters	1978
Newsfront	1978
Kostas	1979
Maybe This Time	1980
Breaker Morant	1980
The Z Men	1980
Heatwave	1981
The Man from Snowy River	1982
The Return of Captain Invincible	1982
Lonely Hearts	1983
Razorback	1983
Freedom	1983
Return to Eden	1984
Man of Flowers	1984
The Coca Cola Kid	1984
A Street to Die	1985
Burke and Wills	1985
Wills and Burke	1985
Strikebound	1985
The Clinic	1985
Malcolm	1986
Double Skulls	1986
Dogs in Space	1986
The Talk of Ruby Rose	1986
The Bit Part	1987
Warm Nights on a Slow Train	1987
The First Kangaroos	1987
The Navigator: A Medieval Odyssey	1987

O. P. HEGGIE (1876-1936)

Character actor of stage and screen in Hollywood, popular
during the thirties.

The Actress	1928
The Letter	1929
Mysterious Dr. Fu Manchu	1929
The Wheel of Life	1929
Broken Dishes	1930
Playboy of Paris	1930
Sunny	1930
The Mighty	1930
Vagabond King	1930
The Return of Dr. Fu Manchu	1930
The Bad Man	1930
One Romantic Night	1930
The Woman Between	1931
Devotion	1931
Too Young to Marry	1931
East Lynne	1931
Smilin' Through	1932
The King's Vacation	1933
Zoo in Budapest	1933
Anne of Green Gables	1934
The Count of Monte Cristo	1934
Peck's Bad Boy	1934
Midnight	1934
Chasing Yesterday	1935
A Dog of Flanders	1935
Return of Frankenstein	1935
Ginger	1935
The Bride of Frankenstein	1935
The Prisoner of Shark Island	1936

SIR ROBERT HELPMANN (1909–1986)

Distinguished Australian character actor and ballet star, in occasional films; also stage star and choreographer.

One of Our Aircraft Is Missing	1942
Henry V	1944
Caravan	1946
The Red Shoes	1948
Tales of Hoffman	1951
Two for Tea	1953
The Iron Petticoat	1956
The Big Money	1956
55 Days at Peking	1962

The Soldier's Tale	1964
The Quiller Memorandum	1966
Chitty Chitty Bang Bang	1968
Alice's Adventures in Wonderland	1972
Don Quixote	1973
The Mango Tree	1977
Puzzle	1978
Patrick	1979
Second Time Lucky	1984
That's Dancing	1985
A Country Practice	1986

ANOUSKA HEMPEL (1949-)

New Zealand actress of stage, screen, and much TV.

On Her Majesty's Secret Service	1969
Scars of Dracula	1970
The Magnificent 7 Deadly Sins	1971
Go for a Take	1972
Tiffany Jones	1973
Black Snake	1973
Slaves	1973
Harriet's Back in Town	1974
So It Goes	1974
The Doll	1975
Time and Again	1975
The Ski Boy	1976
Double Exposure	1976
Return of the Saint	1977
Lady Oscar	1978

PAUL HOGAN (1942-)

Australian leading man of the eighties who gained international success through TV ads; also an enormous success initially in films.

Crocodile Dundee	1986
Anzacs	1987
Australia Live	1987
Crocodile Dundee II	1988

HAROLD HOPKINS

Australian supporting and leading actor of films and television.

Age of Consent	1969
Demonstrator	1972
Picture Show Man	1978
The Club	1980
Gallipoli	1981
Monkey Grip	1981
Ginger Meggs	1982
The Winds of Jarrah	1983
Buddies	1984
The Highest Honour	1984
Fantasy Man	1985
Top Kid	1986
Fields of Fire	1987
The Year My Voice Broke	1987

JOHN HOWARD

Australian character actor of stage and screen, not to be confused with the American actor of the same name.

The Lamp Still Burns	1943
Twilight Hour	1944
Waltz Time	1945
The Way to the Stars	1945
Beware of Pity	1946
The Overlanders	1946
The White Unicorn	1947
The Queen of Spades	1949
The Dancing Years	1950
The Cruel Sea	1953
The Sky Bike	1967
Razorback	1983
Bush Christmas	1984
The Highest Honour	1985
Strikebound	1985
Around the World in 80 Ways	1986
Resoration Piece	1986

WENDY HUGHES

Attractive, prominent Australian leading lady of stage, screen
and television of the 1970s and 1980s.

Touch of Revenge	1972
The Company Men	1972
Rush	1973
The Outsiders	1974
Numbers 96	1974
Eye of the Spiral	1975
Is Anybody There?	1975
Sidecar Racers	1975
Jock Petersen	1975
Obsession	1976
Power Without Glory	1976
Homicide	1976
Matlock	1976
High Rolling	1977
The Puzzle	1977
Woman of the House	1978
Patrol Boat	1978
The Alternative	1978
Newsfront	1978
Kostas	1979
Coralie Lansdowne Says No	1979
Lucinda Brayford	1979
Touch and Go	1980
My Brilliant Career	1980
For a Child Called Michael	1980
A Burning Man	1981
Hoodwink	1981
Partners	1982
A Dangerous Summer	1982
Lonely Hearts	1983
Careful He Might Hear You	1983
My First Wife	1984
Return to Eden	1984
Remember Me	1985
Happy New Year	1985
An Indecent Obsession	1985
I Can't Get Started	1985
Promises to Keep	1986
Amerika	1986
Warm Nights on a Slow Train	1987

Shadows of the Peacock   1987
Boundaries of the Heart   1987

BARRY HUMPHRIES (1934-)

Australian actor in occasional films, notable for his one-man
shows and creation of character Dame Edna Everage. Much TV.

Bedazzled   1967
The Bliss of Mrs. Blossom   1968
The Adventures of Barry McKenzie   1972
Barry McKenzie Holds His Own   1974
Percy's Progress   1974
Side by Side   1975
Pleasure at Her Majesty's   1976
The Getting of Wisdom   1979
Shock Treatment   1982
Les Patterson Saves the World   1987
The Marsupials   1987

BILL HUNTER

Prominent Australian actor of motion pictures and television.

Stone   1974
The Man from Hong Kong   1975
27A   1975
Eliza Fraser   1976
Mad Dog Morgan   1976
Backroads   1977
In Search of Anna   1977
Newsfront   1978
Weekend of Shadows   1979
Hard Knocks   1980
Sam   1980
Heatwave   1981
Maybe This Time   1981
Gallipoli   1981
The Return of Captain Invincible   1982
Far East   1983
Street Hero   1984
No Name No Pack Drill   1985
The Hit   1985

Leonski--The Brown Out Murders	1985
The Last Bastion	1985
An Indecent Obsession	1985
Rebel	1985
The Flying Doctors	1986
Sky Pirates	1986
A Fortunate Life	1986
Death of a Soldier	1986
Fever	1987

ELLIS IRVING (1902-   )

Australian character performer of stage and screen, married to Sophie Stewart. Also Hollywood.

The Bermondsey Kid	1933
Nine Forty-Five	1934
Murder at Monte Carlo	1935
The Black Mask	1935
As You Like It	1936
Member of the Jury	1937
The Sea Hawk	1940
Variety Jubilee	1943
Strawberry Roan	1945
Murder in Reverse	1945
I'll Turn to You	1946
Green Fingers	1947
The Plymouth Adventure	1952
Rough Shoot	1953
Strictly Confidential	1959

ALFRED JAMES (1865-1946)

Australian character player in Hollywood during the 1930s with stage and vaudeville experience.

Everything's Rosie	1931
Heaven on Earth	1931
Thrill Hunters	1933
Hocus Focus	1933
Rocky Rhodes	1934
Six of a Kind	1934
Wonder Bar	1934

Most Precious Things in Life	1934
Elmer and Elsie	1934
Cockeyed Cavaliers	1934
Dr. Socrates	1935
The Great Ziegfeld	1936
The Singing Cowboy	1936
Next Time We Love	1936

JOHN JARRATT

Australian actor, sometimes leading man, of films and TV of the 1970s and 1980s.

Picnic at Hanging Rock	1976
The Great McCarthy	1976
Little Boy Lost	1977
The Odd Angry Shot	1978
Summer City	1979
Long Weekend	1979
The Chant of Jimmie Blacksmith	1980
The Sound of Love	1980
Next of Kin	1982
We of the Never Never	1983
Fluteman	1983
The Settlement	1984
Chase Through the Night	1985
The Naked Country	1985
Palace of Dreams	1985
Dark Age	1986
Melinda	1987

MARGARET JOHNSTON (1918-)

Attractive Australian leading lady and latterly character actress also on stage from 1936.

The Prime Minister	1941
The Rake's Progress	1945
A Man About the House	1947
Portrait of Clare	1950
The Magic Box	1951
Knave of Hearts	1954
Touch and Go	1955

Night of the Eagle	1962
The Model Murder Case	1963
The Nose on My Face	1964
Life at the Top	1965
The Psychopath	1966
Schizo	1966
Sebastian	1967

CLARISSA KAYE

Australian supporting actress of films and TV; widow of James Mason.

Age of Consent	1969
Adam's Woman	1970
Ned Kelly	1970
Frankenstein: The True Story	1973
Dr. Fischer of Geneve	1984
The Good Wife	1986

HUGH KEAYS-BYRNE

Australian character actor of films and television, sometimes in kindly roles.

Stone	1974
The Man from Hong Kong	1975
Mad Dog Morgan	1976
Blue Fin	1978
Mad Max	1979
Snapshot	1979
Chain Reaction	1980
Toby and the Koala Bear	1982
Strikebound	1984
Where the Green Ants Dream	1985
Les Patterson Saves the World	1987

JUDY KELLY (1913-)

Australian leading lady of films, popular during the thirties.

Adam's Apple	1928

Sleepless Nights	1931
Money Talks	1932
Lord Camber's Ladies	1932
Their Night Out	1933
Hawleys of High Street	1933
The Love Nest	1933
Private Life of Henry VIII	1933
Crime on the Hill	1933
Mannequin	1933
The Black Abbot	1934
Four Masked Men	1934
Anything Might Happen	1934
It's a Bet	1935
Things Are Looking Up	1935
Royal Cavalcade	1935
Marry the Girl	1935
Charing Cross Road	1935
Captain Bill	1935
Under Proof	1936
First Offence	1936
A Star Fell From Heaven	1936
The Limping Man	1936
Ship's Concert	1937
Aren't Men Beasts?	1937
Over She Goes	1937
Boys Will Be Girls	1937
The Price of Folly	1937
Make Up	1937
The Last Chance	1937
Premiere	1938
Luck of the Navy	1938
Jane Steps Out	1938
Queer Cargo	1938
At the Villa Rose	1939
Dead Man's Shoes	1939
The Midas Touch	1939
Saloon Bar	1940
George and Margaret	1940
Tomorrow We Live	1942
The Butler's Dilemma	1943
It Happened One Sunday	1944
Dead of Night	1945
Dancing with Crime	1947
Warning to Wantons	1948

GERARD KENNEDY

Australian Actor of stage, occasional features, and television.

Eliza Fraser	1976
The Mango Tree	1977
Puzzle	1977
Newsfront	1978
The Irishman	1978
Raw Deal	1979
Last of the Knucklemen	1980
Fatty Finn	1981
The Plains of Heaven	1983
Flight into Hell	1985
Golden Pennies	1985
Against the Wind	1985
Stock Squad	1986
The Lighthorsemen	1987

GRAHAM KENNEDY

Australian actor of stage, television, and occasional motion
pictures.

The Box	1975
Don's Party	1976
The Odd Angry Shot	1979
The Club	1980
Return of Captain Invincible	1982
Silent Reach	1983
The Killing Fields	1984
Stanley	1985
Travelling North	1986
Les Patterson Saves the World	1987

BILL KERR (1922-)

Balding Australian character star and supporting actor of films
and TV.

Harmony Row	1934
The Silence of Dean Maitland	1935
Penny Points to Paradise	1951

My Death Is a Mockery	1952
Appointment in London	1953
You Know What Sailors Are	1954
The Night My Number Came Up	1955
The Dam Busters	1955
Port of Escape	1956
The Shiralee	1957
The Captain's Table	1959
A Pair of Briefs	1962
The Wrong Arm of the Law	1962
Doctor in Distress	1963
Doctor in Clover	1965
A Funny Thing Happened on the Way to the Forum	1966
Ghost in the Noonday Sun	1973
House of Mortal Sin	1975
Tiffany Jones	1975
Girls Come First	1976
Save the Lady	1981
Gallipoli	1981
Deadline	1981
The Year of Living Dangerously	1982
The Pirate Movie	1982
The Settlement	1983
Dusty	1983
Great Expectations (voice)	1983
Razorback	1983
Platypus Cove	1983
Return to Eden	1983
Vigil	1984
The Coca Cola Kid	1984
The Glitter Dome	1984
Relatives	1985
White Man's Legend	1985
Comedy	1985
Double Skulls	1986
A Fortunate Life	1986
The Lighthorsemen	1987

JOHN KIRBY (1932-1973)

Australian stage and TV actor in some rare films (in Hollywood).

Zorro's Black Whip	1944

Sepia Cinderella	1947
Air Strike	1955
Annapolis Story	1955
Custer of the West	1968
The Royal Hunt of the Sun	1969

LLOYD LAMBLE (1914-   )

Australian character player of stage (from 1934) and films,
usually cast as a policeman, civil servant, etc.; mainly active
during the 1950s. Also pianist.

Saturday Island	1952
Lady in the Fog	1952
Come Back Peter	1952
Curtain Up	1952
Appointment in London	1953
Gilbert and Sullivan	1953
Street Corner	1953
Mantrap	1953
Three Steps to the Gallows	1953
Background	1953
The Straw Man	1953
The Red Dress	1954
Fatal Journey	1954
The Mirror and Markheim	1954
The Green Buddha	1954
Profile	1954
The Belles of St. Trinian's	1954
White Fire	1954
Track the Man Down	1955
The Silent Witness	1955
Out of the Clouds	1955
The Dam Busters	1955
The Girl in the Picture	1956
Person Unknown	1956
Private's Progress	1956
The Man Who Knew Too Much	1956
The Gelignite Gang	1956
The Man Who Never Was	1956
These Dangerous Years	1957
The Good Companions	1957
Night of the Demon	1957
Suspended Alibi	1957

Quatermass II	1957
Barnacle Bill	1957
Seawife	1957
There's Always a Thursday	1957
Blue Murder at St. Trinian's	1958
The Bank Raiders	1958
The Man Who Wouldn't Talk	1958
Dunkirk	1958
No Trees in the Street	1959
Heart of a Man	1959
Our Man in Havana	1959
Breakout	1959
Expresso Bongo	1959
The Challenge	1960
The Trials of Oscar Wilde	1960
The Pure Hell of St. Trinian's	1960
Where I Live	1960
Term of Trial	1962
The Boys	1962
Tiara Tahiti	1963
No Sex Please We're British	1973
And Now the Screaming Starts	1973
On the Game	1974
The Naked Civil Servant	1975
Eskimo Nell	1977
Suez 1956	1979
Very Like a Whale	1980
Peril at Eva House	1982
A Touch of Spring	1982
A Christmas Carol	1983
A Marvellous Profession	1983
Sorry You Never Can Tell	1984
Night Shade	1984
Only Truth Will Serve	1985
Man in a Fog	1985
Me and My Girl	1985
Howard's Way	1986
Body Beautiful	1986

JAMES LAURENSON

New Zealand supporting performer who also appears on television.

Women in Love	1969
The Magic Christian	1970
Assault	1970
Richard II	1970
Edward II	1971
The Exiles	1971
Elizabeth R	1972
The Turn of the Screw	1974
The Prison	1975
Children of the Sun	1976
Esther Waters	1977
Monster Club	1980
A Spy at Evening	1981
Pink Floyd--The Wall	1983
Heartbreakers	1984
Paint Me a Murder	1985
Boney	1985
The Rude Awakening	1986
The Outsiders	1986
The Man Who Fell to Earth	1987
The Bretts	1987

BRYAN LAWRENCE (1909-1983)

Australian singer immensely popular on radio in the thirties; appeared in several films. Also band leader and violinist.

She Shall Have Music	1935
Fame	1936
Sing As You Swing	1937

GEORGE LAZENBY (1939-   )

Australian leading man in international films; his career has been somewhat disappointing after a promising start as James Bond.

On Her Majesty's Secret Service	1969
Universal Soldier	1971
The Dragon Flies	1974
The Man from Hong Kong	1975
Is There Anybody There?	1976
Kentucky Fried Movie	1977
Cover Girls	1977

Death Dimension	1978
Evening in Byzantium	1978
Saint Jack	1979
Stoner	1979
Return of the Man from UNCLE	1983
The Newman Shame	1984
Rituals	1985
Never Too Young to Die	1986

JOHN LEE (1928-   )

Australian supporting performer with radio experience; also much on stage and television.

Dunkirk	1958
Cat Girl	1958
The Silent Enemy	1958
The Flying Scot	1958
The Gypsy and the Gentleman	1959
Under Ten Flags	1960
The Liar	1960
Seven Keys	1961
The Secret Partner	1961
Dr. Crippen	1962
A Stitch in Time	1963
Go Kart Go!	1964
Spaceflight IC1	1965
Crossplot	1969
Say Hello to Yesterday	1970
Double Exposure	1976
Sky Pirates	1977
ffolkes	1980
A Town Like Alice	1981

MARK LEE

Young Australian leading actor of the eighties.

Gallipoli	1981
The Best of Friends	1982
The City's Edge	1984
Emma's War	1986
The Nuclear Conspiracy	1986
The Everlasting Secret Family	1987

DENNIS LILL (1942-)

Balding New Zealand supporting actor primarily seen on television; occasional films.

Fall of Eagles	1974
The Case of Eliza Armstrong	1975
Madame Bovary	1976
Lillie	1978
Hedda Gabler	1979
Bad Blood	1982
The Scarlet Pimpernel	1982
Arthur the King	1983
Partners in Crime	1984
Florence Nightingale	1985
The Innocent	1985
Jenny's War	1985
Mapp and Lucia	1986

MARIE LOHR (1890-1975)

Australian actress of stage (from 1901) and screen, usually seen in dignified or aristocratic roles.

The Real Thing at Last	1916
Aren't We All	1932
Road House	1934
My Heart is Calling	1934
Lady in Danger	1934
Foreign Affaires	1935
Royal Cavalcade	1935
Fighting Stock	1935
Cock O' the North	1935
Whom the Gods Love	1936
It's You I Want	1936
Dreams Come True	1936
Reasonable Doubt	1936
Oh Daddy!	1936
South Riding	1938
Pygmalion	1938
A Gentleman's Gentleman	1939
George and Margaret	1940
Major Barbara	1941
Went the Day Well?	1942

Twilight Hour	1944
Kiss the Bride Goodbye	1944
The Rake's Progress	1945
The Magic Bow	1947
Ghosts of Berkeley Square	1947
Counterblast	1948
Anna Karenina	1948
The Winslow Boy	1948
Silent Dust	1949
Treasure Hunt	1950
Playbill	1951
Little Big Shot	1952
The Devil's Plot	1953
Always a Bride	1953
Out of the Clouds	1955
Escapade	1955
A Town Like Alice	1956
On Such a Night	1956
Seven Waves Away	1957
Small Hotel	1957
Carleton Browne of the FO	1959
Great Catharine	1968

REG LYE

Australian character actor of films and television, sometimes in cameo roles.

King of the Coral Sea	1954
Smiley	1956
The Shiralee	1957
Smiley Gets a Gun	1958
The Wrong Arm of the Law	1962
The Amorous Prawn	1962
King Rat	1965
The Wrong Box	1966
Fathom	1967
A Challenge For Robin Hood	1967
Danger Route	1967
The Lost Continent	1968
The Games	1970
10 Rillington Place	1971
Dracula	1973
Spell of Evil	1973

The Chiffy Kids   1976
Blind Man's Bluff   1977
Wombling Free   1978
Tarka the Otter   1979
The Spaceman & King Arthur   1979
A Man Called Intrepid   1979
The Killing of Angel Street   1981
Sunday Too Far Away   1982
Molly   1983
Freedom   1983
The Boy in the Bush   1984

JOHN MCCALLUM (1917-)

Australian leading actor of stage (from 1934) and films, married
to Googie Withers.

Heritage   1935
South West Pacific   1936
Joe Come Back   1936
Joe Goes Back   1944
Australia Is Like This   1944
A Son Is Born   1945
Bush Christmas   1947
The Root of All Evil   1947
The Loves of Joanna Godden   1947
It Always Rains On Sunday   1947
Miranda   1948
The Calendar   1948
A Boy, a Girl, and a Bike   1949
Traveller's Joy   1949
The Woman in Question   1950
Valley of the Eagles   1951
The Magic Box   1951
Lady Godiva Rides Again   1951
Derby Day   1952
Trent's Last Case   1952
Melba   1953
The Long Memory   1953
Devil on Horseback   1954
Trouble in the Glen   1954
Port of Escape   1955
Smiley   1956
Safe Harbour   1957
Hotel Du Lac   1985

BETTY MCDOWALL

Australian actress seen in occasional films, and also on stage and TV.

The Shiralee	1957
Time Lock	1957
She Didn't Say No	1958
Jack the Ripper	1959
Jackpot	1960
Spare the Rod	1961
Tomorrow at Ten	1962
Echo of Diana	1963
First Men in the Moon	1964
Ballad in Blue	1965
The Liquidator	1966
The Omen	1976

JOHN P. MCGOWAN (1880-1952)

Australian actor of stage and screen, also director, producer, and screenwriter. In Hollywood.

From the Manger to the Cross	1912
Hazards of Helen	1915
The Railroad Raiders	1917
Do or Die	1921
Discontented Wives	1921
Cold Steel	1921
A Crook's Romance	1921
The White Horseman	1921
King of the Circus	1921
Hills of Missing Men	1922
Reckless Chances	1922
The Ruse of the Rattler	1922
The Whipping Boss	1923
One Million in Jewels	1923
Stormy Seas	1923
Crossed Trails	1924
A Two-Fisted Tenderfoot	1924
Barriers of the Law	1924
Boarder Intrigue	1925
Crack O' Dawn	1925
Duped	1925

The Fear Fighter	1925
Makers of Men	1925
Outwitted	1925
Blood and Steel	1925
The Fighting Sheriff	1925
Danger Quest	1926
Moran of the Mounted	1926
The Patent Leather Kid	1926
Red Blood	1926
Senor Daredevil	1926
The Ace of Clubs	1926
The Lost Express	1926
Arizona Nights	1927
Gun Gospel	1927
The Lost Limited	1927
Red Signals	1927
The Red Raiders	1927
The Slaver	1927
Whispering Smith Rides	1927
The Royal American	1927
Tarzan & the Golden Lion	1927
The Black Ace	1928
Arizona Days	1928
The Code of the Scarlet	1928
Devil Dogs	1928
Devil's Tower	1928
Dugan of the Dugouts	1928
Headin' Westward	1928
Law of the Mounted	1928
Lightning Shot	1928
The Old Code	1928
On the Divide	1928
Ships of the Night	1928
Silent Trail	1928
Texas Tommy	1928
The Two Outlaws	1928
West of Santa Fe	1928
Painted Trail	1928
Chinatown Mystery	1928
Senor Americano	1928
The Phantom Raider	1929
The Invaders	1929
Fighting Terror	1929
Oklahoma Kid	1929
Bad Man's Money	1929

The Cleanup	1929
Below the Deadline	1929
A Lawless Legion	1929
Captain Cowboy	1929
The Lone Horseman	1929
The Silent Trail	1929
The Last Roundup	1929
The Golden Bridle	1929
Ships of the Night	1929
Plunging Hoofs	1929
Riders of the Rio Grande	1929
Neath Western Skies	1929
The Cowboy & the Outlaw	1930
Pioneers of the West	1930
Canyon of Missing Men	1930
Covered Wagon Trails	1930
O' Malley Rides Alone	1930
Breezy Bill	1930
Near the Rainbow's End	1930
Riders of the North	1931
Hurricane Express	1932
Somewhere in Arizona	1933
When a Man Rides Alone	1933
The Red Rider	1934
No More Women	1934
Wagon Wheels	1934
Fighting Hero	1934
Rustlers of Red Dog	1935
Mississippi	1935
Boarder Brigands	1935
Bar 20 Rides Again	1935
Stampede	1936
Guns & Guitars	1936
The 3 Mesqueeters	1936
Secret Patrol	1936
Ride 'em Cowboy	1936
Fury and the Woman	1937
Hit the Saddle	1937
Heart of the Rockies	1937
Slave Ship	1937
The Great Adventures of Wild Bill	
Hickok	1938
The Buccaneer	1938
Kennedy's Castle	1938
Hunted Men	1938

In Old Montana	1939
Code of the Fearless	1939
Calling All Marines	1939
Stagecoach	1939

ANGELA PUNCH MCGREGOR

Australian leading actress of films and TV of the eighties.

Newsfront	1978
The Chant of Jimmie Blacksmith	1980
The Survivor	1981
The Best of Friends	1982
Double Deal	1982
We of the Never Never	1983
Annie	1984
The Hunchback of Notre Dame	1985
A Test of Love	1985
Whose Baby?	1986
Double Skulls	1986
Tusitala	1986

LEO MCKERN (1920-   )

Canny, corpulent Australian character star of stage (1944)
and screen, also in Hollywood. Also outstanding as lawyer
Horace Rumpole in Rumpole of the Bailey (1979-81) on television.

Murder in the Cathedral	1952
All for Mary	1955
X the Unknown	1956
Time Without Pity	1957
A Tale of Two Cities	1958
Beyond This Place	1959
Yesterday's Enemy	1959
The Mouse That Roared	1959
Scent of Mystery	1960
Jazzboat	1960
The Running, Jumping, & Standing Still Film	1960
Mikhali (voice)	1960
The Day the Earth Caught Fire	1961

Mr. Topaze	1962
The Inspector	1962
Private Potter	1962
The Horse Without a Head	1963
Doctor in Distress	1963
Hot Enough For June	1963
A Jolly Bad Fellow	1964
King and Country	1964
Moll Flanders	1965
Help!	1965
The Drinking Party	1965
Alice in Wonderland	1966
A Man for All Seasons	1966
Assignment K	1967
Decline and Fall	1968
The Shoes of the Fisherman	1968
Nobody Runs Forever	1968
On the Eve of Publication	1968
Ryan's Daughter	1970
Massacre in Rome	1973
Afternoon at the Festival	1973
Penda's Fen	1974
Adventures of Sherlock Holmes' Smarter Brother	1975
The Omen	1976
Cadleshoe	1978
The Nativity	1978
Our Mutual Friend	1978
Damien: Omen II	1978
The House On Garibaldi Street	1979
The Last Tasmanian (voice)	1979
The Lion, the Witch and the Wardrobe (voice)	1979
The Blue Lagoon	1980
The French Lieutenant's Woman	1981
Rumpole's Return	1982
King Lear	1982
Voyage of Bounty's Child	1983
Reilly, Ace of Spies	1983
Country	1983
Ladyhawke	1984
The Chain	1985
Murder with Mirrors	1985
Monseignor Quixote	1985
Travelling North	1986
Planter of Mulatta	1987

KRIS MCQUADE

Australian actress of the 1970s and 1980s in occasional films; also TV.

Alvin Purple	1973
Alvin Rides Again	1974
The Firm Man	1975
Eskimo Nell	1976
Harvest of Hate	1977
Kostas	1980
Fighting Back	1983
Buddies	1984
The Coca Cola Kid	1984
The Surfer	1986
Fields of Fire	1987
Two Friends	1987

JOAN MARION (1908-)

Popular Australian actress of the thirties, also seen on stage (from 1925).

Her Night Out	1932
Little Fella	1932
The River House Ghost	1932
The Stolen Necklace	1933
Out of the Past	1933
The Melody Maker	1933
Double Wedding	1933
Going Straight	1933
Lord of the Manor	1933
Tangled Evidence	1934
Sensation	1937
For Valour	1937
Black Limelight	1938
Premiere	1938
Spies of the Air	1939
Dead Man's Shoes	1939
Ten Days in Paris	1939
Trio	1950
Tons of Trouble	1956

ALAN MARSHAL (1909-1961)

Australian light romantic leading man of the 1930s and 1940s in Hollywood, also on stage.

The Garden of Allah	1936
After the Thin Man	1936
Night Must Fall	1937
Parnell	1937
Conquest	1937
Robber Symphony	1937
The Road to Reno	1938
Dramatic School	1938
Invisible Enemy	1938
I Met My Love Again	1938
The Hunchback of Notre Dame	1939
The Adventures of Sherlock Holmes	1939
Exile Express	1939
Four Girls in White	1939
Tom, Dick, and Harry	1940
Married and in Love	1940
Irene	1940
The Howards of Virginia	1940
He Stayed for Breakfast	1940
Lydia	1941
Bride by Mistake	1944
The White Cliffs of Dover	1944
The Barkleys of Broadway	1948
The Opposite Sex	1956
The House on Haunted Hill	1959
Day of the Outlaw	1959

MURRAY MATHESON (1912-1985)

Quiet, pleasant-mannered Australian character actor of stage, films, and television; in Hollywood from early 1950s. TV series: Banacek (1972-74) (as Felix Mulholland).

The Way to the Stars	1945
Journey Together	1945
The Secret Tunnel	1947
The Fool and the Princess	1948
Hurricane Smith	1952
The Plymouth Adventure	1952

Botany Bay	1953
King of the Khyber Rifles	1953
Flight to Tangier	1953
Jamaica Run	1953
The Ganeston Chronicle	1954
Love Is a Many Splendored Thing	1955
The Bamboo Curtain	1955
The Canary Sedan	1958
The Moon and Sixpence	1959
The Poisoner	1960
Letter to a Lover	1961
The Throwback	1961
Five Characters in Search of an Exit	1962
Wall of Noise	1963
Murder Case	1964
Signpost to Murder	1965
Assult on a Queen	1966
How to Succeed in Business	1967
In Enemy Country	1968
Star!	1968
Explosion	1970
Lieutenant Schuster's Wife	1971
Detour to Nowhere	1972
The Greatest Collection of Them All	1972
Let's Hear It for a Living Legend	1972
A Million the Hard Way	1972
No Sign of the Cross	1972
Project Phoenix	1972
To Steal a King	1973
The 2 Million Clams of Capt. Jack	1973
Ten Thousand Dollars a Page	1973
A Horse of a Slightly Different Colour	1973
If Max Is So Smart, Who Doesn't He Tell Us Where He Is?	1973
Rocket to Oblivion	1974
Fly Me--If You Can Find Me	1974
No Stone Unturned	1974
Now You See It, Now You Don't	1974
The Three Million Dollar Piracy	1974
The Vanishing Chalice	1975
Tail Gunner Joe	1977
Rabbit Test	1978
Mary and Joseph	1980
The Million Dollar Face	1981
Kiss of Gold	1981

Angel on My Shoulder	1981
The Lover	1981
The Great Detective	1982
Twilight Zone--The Movie	1983

RAY MEAGHER

Australian stage and television actor who has had some noteworthy film appearances as well.

Money Movers	1978
The Journalist	1978
My Brilliant Career	1979
The Odd Angry Shot	1979
The Chant of Jimmie Blacksmith	1980
Breaker Morant	1980
On the Run	1983
Mail Order Bride	1984
Mystery at Castle Cove	1985
Short Changed	1985
On the Loose	1985
A Fortunate Life	1986
Dark Age	1986
Five Times Dizzy	1986
Blue Lightning	1987
The Place at the Coast	1987
Colour in the Creek	1987

JOHN MEILLON (1933-)

Australian character actor and supporting performer of films
and television.

On the Beach	1959
The Sundowners	1960
The Long & the Short & the Tall	1961
Offbeat	1961
Watch It Sailor	1961
Operation Snatch	1962
Billy Budd	1962
Death Trap	1962
The Valiant	1962
The Longest Day	1962

The Running Man	1963
Cairo	1963
Guns at Batasi	1964
633 Squadron	1964
Dead Man's Chest	1965
They're a Weird Mob	1966
Outback	1970
Walkabout	1971
Susnstuck	1972
The Dove	1974
Inn of the Damned	1974
Sidecar Racers	1975
Ride a Wild Pony	1975
The Cars That Eat People	1976
The Fourth Wish	1977
Born to Run	1977
The Picture Show Man	1978
Timelapse	1980
Heatwave	1981
The Dismissal	1983
The Wild Duck	1983
The Camel Boy	1983
Scales of Justice	1984
The Man in the Iron Mask	1985
Crocodile Dundee	1986
Frenchman's Farm	1986
Blue Lightning	1986
The Dunera Boys	1986
The Everlasting Secret Family	1987
Bullseye	1987

KEITH MICHELL (1926-   )

Australian leading man of stage (1947), screen, and television; former art teacher.

True As a Turtle	1957
Dangerous Exile	1957
The Gypsy and the Gentleman	1958
The Hellfire Club	1961
All Night Long	1962
Antony and Cleopatra	1962
Seven Seas to Calais	1963
House of Cards	1968

Prudence and the Pill	1968
The Executioner	1970
An Ideal Husband	1971
The Six Wives of Henry VIII	1972
Henry VIII and His Six Wives	1972
Moments	1973
The Story of Jacob and Joseph	1974
The Story of David	1976
The Tenth Month	1979
Julius Caesar	1979
The Day Christ Died	1980
Grendel Grendel Grendel	1982
The Gondoliers	1984
The Pirates of Penzance	1985
My Brother Tom	1986
The First Fleet	1987
The Wind and the Stars	1987
Captain Cook	1987

DENNIS MILLER

Australian television and occasional motion picture performer.

Alvin Purple	1973
The Great McCarthy	1975
Eliza Fraser	1976
The Journalist	1979
Last of the Knucklemen	1980
Stir	1980
Hoodwink	1981
Heatwave	1981
Starstruck	1983
Silver City	1985
The Other Facts of Life	1986
Colour in the Creek	1987
The Petrov Affair	1987

RICHARD MOIR

Australian actor of the seventies and eighties, also much on TV.

27A	1976
In Search of Anna	1978
The Odd Angry Shot	1979

Chain Reaction	1980
Heatwave	1981
Sweet Dreamers	1981
Running on Empty	1982
The Plains of Heaven	1984
Singles	1984
An Indecent Obsession	1985
The Long Way Home	1985
The Wrong World	1985
Land of Hope	1986
The Challenge	1986
Pandemonium	1987
Jilted	1987

GEORGE MOON (1886-1968)

Australian character actor who made occasional films; also on stage.

Diggers	1933
A Co-respondent's Course	1933
Soldiers Don't Care	1934
Lightning Conductor	1938
Me and My Pal	1939
Time Flies	1944
What Do We Do Now?	1945
An Alligator Named Daisy	1955
It's a Wonderful World	1956
Davy	1957
Carry On Admiral	1957
Breath of Life	1962
A Matter of Choice	1963
The Boys	1963
Promise Her Anything	1965
Monster of Terror	1966
Half a Sixpence	1967
Bachelor of Arts	1969

JUDY MORRIS

Fascinating Australian leading actress of films and television.

Three to Go	1971

The Child	1972
Between Wars	1974
The Great McCarthy	1975
Scobie Malone	1975
The Trespassers	1976
In Search of Anna	1977
Picture Show Man	1978
The Plumber	1979
Maybe This Time	1981
Phar Lap	1983
Razorback	1984
The Last Frontier	1986
Colour in the Creek	1987
Ring of Scorpio	1987

HELEN MORSE

Pretty Australian leading lady of films and television.

Australian Playhouse	1972
Homicide	1972
Division 4	1973
Marion	1974
Stone	1974
Jock Petersen	1975
Picnic at Hanging Rock	1976
Caddie	1978
Agatha	1979
A Town Like Alice	1981
Far East	1982
Silent Reach	1983
Iris	1984
Out of Time	1985

HENRY MOWBRAY (1882-1960)

Australian stage actor who made a few films in Hollywood.

Fifty Fathoms Deep	1931
The Pursuit of Happiness	1934
The Leathernecks Have Landed	1936

ROD MULLINAR

Australian supporting and sometimes leading actor of occasional
films.

The Set	1971
Stockade	1973
Raw Deal	1978
Patrick	1979
Thirst	1979
Breaker Morant	1980
Maybe This Time	1981
Partners	1982
Breakfast in Paradise	1983
Five Mile Creek	1984
The Surfer	1986
Shadows of the Peacock	1987

RUSSELL NAPIER (1910-1975)

Australian character star of the fifties and sixties, often seen
as police inspector or other officials.

End of the River	1947
Stolen Face	1952
Blind Man's Bluff	1952
Death of an Angel	1952
Black Orchid	1953
The Unholy Four	1954
The Dark Stairway	1954
The Strange Case of Blondie	1954
Conflict of Wings	1954
Companions in Crime	1954
The Saint's Return	1954
36 Hours	1954
Out of the Clouds	1955
Little Red Monkey	1955
The Brain Machine	1955
Blue Peter	1955
A Time to Kill	1955
A Town Like Alice	1956
The Narrowing Circle	1956
Man in the Road	1956
Guilty	1956

The Last Man to Hang	1956
Destination Death	1956
Person Unknown	1956
The Lonely House	1957
The Shiralee	1957
Robbery Under Arms	1957
The White Cliffs Mystery	1957
Night Crossing	1957
The Case of the Smiling Widow	1957
The Son of Robin Hood	1958
A Night to Remember	1958
Tread Softly Stranger	1958
Crime of Honour	1958
Distant Neighbours (voice)	1958
The Witness	1959
The Ghost Train Murder	1959
The Unseeing Eye	1959
Hell Is a City	1960
The Last Train	1960
Evidence in Concrete	1960
Sink the Bismarck	1960
The Angry Silence	1960
The Mark	1961
The Grand Junction Case	1961
The Never Never Murder	1961
Barabbas	1961
Francis of Assissi	1961
Fire Below	1962
HMS Defiant	1962
Mix Me a Person	1962
Man in the Middle	1964
It	1966
Blood Beast Terror	1968
Twisted Nerve	1968
Nobody Runs Forever	1968
The Black Windmill	1974

SAM NEILL (1948-)

Versatile New Zealand leading man of films and television
popular in the eighties; married to Lisa Harrow.

Sleeping Dogs	1977
The Journalist	1978

Just Out of Reach	1979
My Brilliant Career	1979
The Z Men	1980
The Final Conflict	1981
From a Far Country	1981
Possession	1982
Ivanhoe	1982
The Enigma	1982
Reilly, Ace of Spies	1983
The Country Girls	1983
The Blood of Others	1984
Robbery Under Arms	1984
Mansfield	1985
Plenty	1985
Kane and Abel	1985
The Umbrella Woman	1986
Strong Medicine	1986
For Love Alone	1986
The Good Wife	1986
Amerika	1987
Dead Calm	1987
Evil Angels	1987

ROBYN NEVIN

Strong Australian leading actress of stage, screen, and television.

The Priest	1972
Libido	1976
The Fourth Wish	1977
The Irishman	1978
Caddie	1978
The Chant of Jimmie Blacksmith	1980
Goodbye Paradise	1982
Tread Softly	1982
Fighting Back	1983
Careful He Might Hear You	1983
For Love or Money	1984
The Coolangatta Gold	1985
Hanlon	1986

MIGNON O'DOHERTY (1890-1961)

Australian actress of stage (from 1913) and occasional motion
pictures.

There Goes the Bride	1932
The Faithful Heart	1932
The Good Companions	1933
Channel Crossing	1933
Autumn Crocus	1934
Dandy Dick	1935
Neutral Port	1940
He Found a Star	1941
Hard Steel	1942
Let the People Sing	1942
The Lamp Still Burns	1943
Maytime in Mayfair	1949
White Corridors	1951
Ghost Ship	1953
You Lucky People	1955
The Whole Truth	1958
Never Let Go	1960

NANCY O'NEIL (1911-)

Australian supporting and also leading actress of stage (since
1931) and screen, popular in the 1930s. Not to be confused
with American actress Nance O'Neil (1874-1965).

The Secret of the Loch	1934
Sometimes Good	1934
Something Always Happens	1934
The Medium	1934
Crazy People	1934
Brewster's Millions	1935
Hello Sweetheart	1935
The Brown Wallet	1936
Twelve Good Men	1936
Educated Evans	1936
Head Office	1936
Fifty Shilling Boxer	1937
The Angelus	1937
There Was a Young Man	1937
East of Ludgate Hill	1937

Darts Are Trumps	1938
Garrison Follies	1940
Somewhere in Civvies	1943
Headline	1943
The Titfield Thunderbolt	1953
Solo for Sparrow	1962

MICHAEL PATE (1920-   )

Australian character actor mainly in Hollywood, often seen as Indian or villain. TV series: <u>Matlock Police</u> (1971).

Forty Thousand Horsemen	1940
The Rugged O'Riordans	1949
Bitter Springs	1950
The Strange Door	1951
Thunder on the Hill	1951
Ten Tall Men	1951
Target Hong Kong	1952
Five Fingers	1952
Face to Face	1952
The Black Castle	1952
Julius Caesar	1953
Houdini	1953
Hondo	1953
Scandal at Scourie	1953
All the Brothers Were Valiant	1953
The Secret Sharer	1953
The Desert Rats	1953
Rogue's March	1953
The Maze	1953
Royal African Rifles	1953
El Alamein	1953
Secret of the Incas	1954
King Richard & the Crusaders	1954
The Silver Chalice	1955
The Lawless Street	1955
African Fury (voice)	1955
The Court Jester	1956
The Killer Is Loose	1956
The Revolt of Mamie Stover	1956
Congo Crossing	1956
The Cavalry	1957
Reprisal	1957

The Tall Stranger	1957
Something of Value	1957
The Oklahoman	1957
Face of Fear	1957
Desert Hell	1958
Hong Kong Confidential	1958
Murder in Gratitude	1958
Green Mansions	1959
Curse of the Undead	1959
Westbound	1959
Zorro the Avenger	1960
Walk Like a Dragon	1960
Trio For Terror	1960
The Canadians	1961
Sergeants Three	1962
Tower of London	1962
Drums of Africa	1963
California	1963
PT 109	1963
McLintock	1963
Beauty and the Beast	1963
Advance to the Rear	1964
The McGregor Affair	1964
Major Dundee	1965
Brainstorm	1965
The Great Sioux Massacre	1965
Thou Still Unravished Bride	1965
Willie and the Yank	1966
Hondo and the Apaches	1966
The Singing Nun	1966
Return of a Gunfighter	1967
Little Jungle Boy	1970
Mad Dog Morgan	1976
Partners	1981
The Return of Captain Invincible	1982
The Wild Duck	1983
The Camel Boy	1984
The Sons of Matthew O'Reilly	1985
Death of a Soldier	1986
Body Business	1986
The Marsupials	1987

VERA PEARCE (1896-1966)

Australian supporting actress and singer, most popular in the thirties.

Yes Mr. Brown	1933
Just My Luck	1933
That's a Good Girl	1933
So You Won't Talk	1935
Yes Madam	1938
What a Man!	1939
Nicholas Nickleby	1947
One Wild Oat	1951
Men of Sherwood Forest	1954
The Night We Dropped a Clanger	1959

WILLIAM PERCY (1872-1946)

Australian character actor who was seen in a few films of the 1930s.

Oh Daddy!	1935
Late Extra	1935
Troubled Waters	1936
Public Nuisance No. 1	1936
Highland Fling	1936
The Black Tulip	1937

MINNA PHILLIPS (1872-1963)

Australian character actress of stage and occasional films in Hollywood.

The Male Animal	1942
A Yank at Eton	1942
My Sister Eileen	1942
Sherlock Holmes Faces Death	1943
Girls Inc.	1943
Hers to Hold	1943
Bandit Queen	1950
Queen for a Day	1951
Strangers on a Train	1951

DAPHNE POLLARD (1890-1978)

Australian actress of stage and screen with vaudeville experience;
filmed in Hollywood.

Hit of the Show	1928
Sinners of Love	1928
Wanted a Man	1928
Cleo to Cleopatra	1928
Big Time	1929
A Perfect Day	1929
The Sky Hawk	1929
South Sea Rose	1929
The Old Barn	1929
What a Widow!	1930
Swing Time	1930
Bright Lights	1930
Loose Ankles	1930
Sugar Plum Papa	1930
Bulls and Bears	1930
Goodbye Legs	1930
Don't Bite Your Dentist	1930
Racket Cheers	1930
The Lady Refuses	1931
Bonnie Scotland	1935
Thicker Than Water	1935
Our Relations	1936
Tillie the Toiler	1941
The Dancing Masters	1943
Kid Dynamite	1943

HARRY POLLARD (1886-1962)

Australian vaudeville comic in Hollywood, nicknamed "Snub."
One of the original keystone cops. A star of silents, latterly
seen in character parts. Not to be confused with director of
the same name (1883-1934).

Great While It Lasted	1915
Start Something	1919
All at Sea	1919
Call for Mr. Cave Man	1919
Giving the Bride Away	1919
Order in Court	1919

It's a Hard Life	1919
How Dry I Am	1919
Looking for Trouble	1919
Tough Luck	1919
The Floor Below	1919
His Royal Slyness	1919
Red Hot Hottentots	1920
Why Go Home	1920
Slippery Slickers	1920
The Dippy Dentist	1920
All Lit Up	1920
Getting His Goat	1920
Waltz Me Around	1920
Raise the Rent	1920
Find the Girl	1920
Fresh Paint	1920
Flat Broke	1920
Cut the Cards	1920
The Dinner Hour	1920
Cracked Wedding Bells	1920
Speed to Spare	1920
Shoot on Sight	1920
Don't Weaken	1920
Drink Hearty	1920
Trotting Through Turkey	1920
All Dressed Up	1920
Grab the Ghost	1920
All in a Day	1920
Any Old Port	1920
Don't Rock the Boat	1920
The Homestretch	1920
Call a Taxi	1920
Live and Learn	1920
Run 'Em Ragged	1920
A London Bobby	1920
Money to Burn	1920
Go As You Please	1920
Rock a Bye Baby	1920
Doing Time	1920
Fellow Citizens	1920
When the Wind Blows	1920
Insulting the Sultan	1920
Dearly Departed	1920
Cash Customers	1920
Park Your Car	1920

The Morning After	1921
Whirl O' the West	1921
Open Another Bottle	1921
His Best Girl	1921
Make It Snappy	1921
Fellow Romans	1921
Rush Order	1921
Bubbling Over	1921
No Children	1921
Own Your Own Home	1921
Big Game	1921
Save Your Money	1921
Blue Sunday	1921
Where's the Fire?	1921
The High Rollers	1921
You're Next	1921
The Bike Bug	1921
At the Ringside	1921
No Stopover	1921
What a Whopper	1921
Teaching the Teacher	1921
Spot Cash	1921
Name the Day	1921
Jail Bird	1921
Late Lodgers	1921
Gone to the Country	1921
Law and Order	1921
15 Minutes	1921
On Location	1921
Hocus-Pocus	1921
Penny-in-the-Slot	1921
The Joy Rider	1921
The Hustler	1921
Sink or Swim	1921
Shake 'Em Up	1921
Corner Pocket	1921
Lose No Time	1922
Call the Witness	1922
Years to Come	1922
Blow 'Em Up	1922
Stage Struck	1922
Down and Out	1922
Pardon Me	1922
The Bow Wows	1922
Hot Off the Press	1922

Anvil Chorus	1922
Jump Your Job	1922
Full O' Pep	1922
Kill the Nerve	1922
Days of Old	1922
Light Showers	1922
Do Me a Favor	1922
In the Movies	1922
Punch the Clock	1922
Strictly Modern	1922
Hale and Hearty	1922
Some Baby	1922
Bed of Roses	1922
The Dumb Bell	1922
The Stone Age	1922
365 Days	1922
Old Sea Dog	1922
Hook Line and Sinker	1922
Nearly Rich	1922
Our Gang	1922
Dig Up	1923
A Tough Winter	1923
Before the Public	1923
Where Am I?	1923
California or Bust	1923
Sold at Auction	1923
Courtship of Miles Sandwich	1923
Jack Frost	1923
The Mystery Man	1923
The Walkout	1923
It's a Gift	1923
Dear Old Pal	1923
Join the Circus	1923
Fully Insured	1923
It's a Boy	1923
The Big Idea	1924
Why Marry?	1924
Get Busy	1924
Are Husbands Human?	1925
Do Your Duty	1926
The Old War Horse	1926
The Doughboy	1926
The Yokel	1926
The Fire	1926
All Wet	1926

The Bum's Rush	1927
Ex-Flame	1931
One Good Turn	1931
The Midnight Patrol	1932
Make Me a Star	1932
Purchase Price	1932
Stingaree	1934
Cockeyed Cavaliers	1934
Just My Luck	1936
The Crime Patrol	1936
The White Legion	1936
Gentleman from Louisiana	1936
Headin for the Rio Grande	1936
Riders of the Rockies	1937
Hittin' the Trail	1937
The Clutching Hand	1937
Nation Aflame	1937
Arizona Days	1937
Tex Rides with the Boy Scouts	1937
Frontier Town	1938
Starlight Over Texas	1938
Where the Buffalo Roam	1938
Song of the Buckaroo	1939
Murder on the Yukon	1940
Phony Express	1943
Defective Detectives	1944
His Tale Is Told	1944
Three Pests in a Mess	1945
Monkey Businessmen	1946
The Perils of Pauline	1947
Blackmail	1948
Loaded Pistols	1949
The Crooked Way	1949
So You Want to Be a Banker	1954
Man of a Thousand Faces	1957
Rock a Bye Baby	1958
Who Was That Lady?	1960
Studs Lonigan	1960
When Comedy Was King	1960
The Errand Boy	1961
Pocketful of Miracles	1962
Days of Thrills & Laughter	1962
30 Years of Fun	1962

NYREE DAWN PORTER (1940-)

Attractive New Zealand leading lady of films and television;
TV series; The Protectors (1972) (as the Contessa).

Sentenced for Life	1960
Identity Unknown	1960
Man at the Carlton Tower	1961
Part Time Wife	1961
Live Now Pay Later	1962
Two Left Feet	1963
The Cracksman	1963
Madame Bovary	1965
The Abbey Grange	1966
The Forsyte Saga	1967
The Gamblers	1968
Jane Eyre	1970
The House That Dripped Blood	1970
Death in Small Doses	1972
From Beyond the Grave	1973
To Die, to Sleep, to Dream	1975
The Martian Chronicles	1980
The Chalk Garden	1985

CHIPS RAFFERTY (1909-1971)

Tall, lanky Australian leading man and latterly character star,
also in Hollywood. Frequently played a variation on a drawling
country type called "Dinkum."

Ants in His Pants	1938
Dan Rudd, MP	1939
Forty Thousand Horsemen	1940
The Rats of Tobruk	1944
Bush Christmas	1945
The Overlanders	1946
The Loves of Joanna Godden	1947
Eureka Stockade	1948
Bitter Springs	1950
Australian Diary	1951
Kangaroo	1952
The Desert Rats	1953
The Phantom Stockman	1953
Cattle Station	1954

King of the Coral Sea	1954
Walk into Hell	1956
Smiley	1956
Smiley Gets a Gun	1958
Power With Precision (voice)	1959
The Sundowners	1960
The Wackiest Ship in the Army	1960
Mutiny on the Bounty	1962
They're a Weird Mob	1966
Double Trouble	1967
Kona Coast	1968
Skulduggery	1970
Outback	1971

LAYA RAKI (1927-)

New Zealand supporting actress of stage and occasionally screen, married to Ron Randell. TV series: <u>Crane</u> (1963).

Up to His Neck	1954
The Seekers	1954
Quentin Durward	1955
The Gallant One	1961
The Beginning Was Sin	1962
The Poppy Is Also a Flower	1965
Savage Pampas	1966
Song of Naples	1968

RON RANDELL (1918-)

Australian leading man and supporting actor of international films and television; former radio star. TV series: <u>O.S.S.</u> (1958). Married to Laya Raki.

The Night of Nights	1939
Pacific Adventure	1946
A Son Is Born	1946
It Had to Be You	1947
Bulldog Drummond at Bay	1947
Sign of the Ram	1948
The Mating of Millie	1948
The Loves of Carmen	1948
Bulldog Drummond Strikes Back	1948

Make Believe Ballroom	1949
Oomo Oomo the Shark God	1949
The Lone Wolf and His Lady	1949
Tyrant of the Sea	1950
Counterspy Meets Scotland Yard	1950
The Corsair	1951
Lorna Doone	1951
The Brigand	1952
Captive Women	1952
Kiss Me Kate	1953
Mississippi Gambler	1953
Girl on the Pier	1953
3000 AD	1953
Ever Since the Day	1953
The Triangle	1953
American Duel	1953
One Just Man	1954
The Apple	1954
The Lovely Place	1954
Desert Sands	1954
Quincannon, Frontier Scout	1955
I Am a Camera	1955
Swamp Mutiny	1955
Bermuda Affair	1956
Count of Twelve	1956
The She-Creature	1956
Beyond Mombasa	1956
The Golden Virgin	1956
The Hostage	1956
Morning Call	1957
The Story of Esther Costello	1957
Girl in Black Stockings	1957
Davy	1957
Man of the Law	1958
Contact	1960
The Most Dangerous Man Alive	1961
King of Kings	1961
The Longest Day	1962
Follow the Boys	1963
Gold For the Caesars	1963
The Phony American	1963
Come Fly with Me	1963
Legend of a Gunfighter	1966
Savage Pampas	1966
Three into Two Won't Go	1969

Whitey	1971
The Seven Minutes	1971
Electra Glide in Blue	1973
Exposed	1983

CAROL RAYE (1923-)

Australian leading actress of the forties in a few films; later in a few more in character roles. Also much stage and TV.

Strawberry Roan	1945
Waltz Time	1945
Spring Song	1946
While I Live	1947
The Journalist	1980
Man of Letters	1984

CLIVE REVILL (1930-)

New Zealand character actor of stage, films, and television, frequently seen in comedy parts. Also latterly in Hollywood.

Reach for the Sky	1956
The Horse's Mouth	1958
The Headless Ghost	1959
Bunny Lake Is Missing	1965
Modesty Blaise	1966
A Fine Madness	1966
Kaleidoscope	1966
Fathom	1967
The Double Man	1967
Once upon a Tractor	1967
Italian Secret Service	1967
The Shoes of the Fisherman	1968
Nobody Runs Forever	1968
The Assassination Bureau	1969
Bam! Pow! Zapp!	1969
The Buttercup Chain	1970
A Severed Head	1970
Private Life of Sherlock Holmes	1970
Rum Runner	1971
Avanti	1971
Escape in the Sun	1972
The Legend of Hell House	1973

The Little Prince	1974
The Black Windmill	1974
The Boy with Two Heads (voice)	1974
Galileo	1975
One of Our Dinosaurs Is Missing	1975
The Great Houdinis	1976
The Conspirators	1976
Winner Take All	1977
Pinocchio	1977
Once upon a Brothers Grimm	1978
Marya	1978
Centennial	1978
Matilda	1978
She's Dressed to Kill	1979
T.R. Sloane	1979
The Scarlett O'Hara War	1980
The Diary of Anne Frank	1980
The Empire Strikes Back (voice)	1980
Charlie Muffin	1980
Death Ray 2000	1981
Zorro the Gay Blade	1981
Samson and Delilah	1983
George Washington	1984
The Ferret	1984
The Mikado	1984
The Sorcerer	1985
Royal Match	1985
Musical Comedy Tonight	1985
A Masterpiece of Murder	1986
Rumplestiltskin	1986
The Frog Prince	1987
The Emperor's New Clothes	1987
Mama's Boy	1987

ANN RICHARDS (1918-1982)

Australian leading actress and second lead, also poet and play-wright. In Hollywood from the forties.

It Isn't Done	1937
Tall Timber	1938
The Rudd Family	1939
Random Harvest	1942
Gillespie's New Assistant	1943
Three Hearts For Julia	1943

An American Romance	1944
Love Letters	1945
Badman's Territory	1946
The Searching Wind	1946
Lost Honeymoon	1947
Love from a Stranger	1947
Sorry Wrong Number	1948
Breakdown	1952

CYRIL RITCHARD (1896-1977)

Australian musical comedy star of stage (from 1917) and screen, also in Hollywood. Former medical student. Also much on TV.

On with the Dance	1927
Piccadilly	1929
Blackmail	1929
Just for a Song	1930
Symphony in Two Flats	1930
Service for Ladies	1932
Danny Boy	1934
It's a Grand Old World	1937
The Show Goes On	1937
Dangerous Medicine	1938
I See Ice	1938
Woman Hater	1948
Ruggles of Red Gap	1951
Mrs. Dane's Defence	1951
Treasure Chest	1952
Pontius Pilate	1952
The 12 Pound Look	1952
Two for One	1953
Here's Father	1954
The King and Mrs. Candle	1954
The Merry Widow	1954
Peter Pan	1955
Visit to a Small Planet	1955
The Spongers	1955
Dearest Enemy	1955
The Good Fairy	1956
Rosalinda	1956
Jack and the Bean Stalk	1956
Caesar and Cleopatra	1956
Aladdin	1958
HMS Pinafore	1959

Peter Pan	1960
The Man Who Bought Paradise	1965
The Dangerous Christmas of Red Rid-	
ing Hood	1965
The Daydreamer (voice)	1966
Half a Sixpence	1967
Hans Brinker	1969
Foul	1970
The Emperor's New Clothes (voice)	1972
Love, Life, Liberty and Lunch	1976
The Hobbit (voice)	1977

MAY ROBSON (1858-1942)

Australian character actress of stage and films, long in Hollywood where she was often seen as forceful but kindly old lady.

How Molly Made Good	1915
A Night Out	1916
His Bridal Night	1919
Broadway Saint	1919
The Last Battalion	1919
Pals in Paradise	1926
A Harp in Hawk	1927
Rubber Tires	1927
King of Kings	1927
Rejuvenation of Aunt Mary	1927
Angel of Broadway	1927
Chicago	1927
The Blue Danube	1928
Turkish Delight	1928
She-Wolf	1931
Mother's Millions	1931
Letty Lynton	1932
Red-Headed Woman	1932
Strange Interlude	1932
If I Had a Million	1932
Little Orphan Annie	1932
Two Against the World	1932
The Engineer's Daughter	1932
Broadway to Hollywood	1933
Men Must Fight	1933
White Sister	1933

Reunion in Vienna	1933
Dancing Lady	1933
Dinner at Eight	1933
One Man's Journey	1933
Lady For a Day	1933
Beauty For Sale	1933
The Solitaire Man	1933
Alice in Wonderland	1933
You Can't Buy Everything	1934
Straight Is the Way	1934
Lady by Choice	1934
Grand Old Girl	1935
Vanessa: Her Love Story	1935
Reckless	1935
Age of Indiscretion	1935
Anna Karenina	1935
Three Kids and a Queen	1935
Strangers All	1935
Mills of the Gods	1935
The Captain's Kid	1936
Wife vs. Secretary	1936
The Baxter Millions	1936
Rainbow on the River	1936
Woman in Distress	1937
Top of the Town	1937
A Star Is Born	1937
The Perfect Specimen	1938
Adventures of Tom Sawyer	1938
Bringing Up Baby	1938
The Texans	1938
Four Daughters	1938
They Made Me a Criminal	1938
Yes My Darling Daughter	1939
The Kid from Kokomo	1939
Daughters Courageous	1939
Nurse Edith Cavell	1939
That's Right You're Wrong	1939
Four Wives	1939
Granny Get Your Gun	1940
Irene	1940
Texas Rangers Ride Again	1941
Four Mothers	1941
Million Dollar Baby	1941
Playmates	1941
Joan of Paris	1942

ALAN ROWE (1926-)

New Zealand supporting and character player with stage,
screen, and television experience.

Taste of Excitement	1969
Say Hello to Yesterday	1970
The First Churchills	1971
Henry VIII & His Six Wives	1972
Waste	1977
The Mayor of Casterbridge	1978
Lillie	1978
In Hiding	1978
Wings of the Dove	1979
Mr. Botibol's First Love	1980
Very Like a Whale	1980
The Tempest	1980
The Member for Chelsea	1981
Death in the Morning	1982
The Last of the Romans	1982
The Witch and the Grinnygog	1983
Morgan's Boy	1984
The First Olympics: Athens 1896	1984
The Shooting Party	1985
Lovejoy	1986
Paradise Postponed	1986
Oedipus the King	1986
First Among Equals	1987

MADGE RYAN (1919-)

Australian supporting actress of occasional films and TV.

The Strange Affair	1968
I Start Counting	1970
A Clockwork Orange	1971
Frenzy	1972
Endless Night	1972
Man and a Snake	1973
Yellow Dog	1973
Who Is Killing the Great Chefs of Europe?	1978
London Belongs to Me	1979
S.O.S. Titanic	1979

The Lady Vanishes	1980
Cymbeline	1982
Bergerac	1983
Heart Attack in a Hotel	1985
Events in a Museum	1985

PAUL SCARDON (1878-1954)

Australian actor of stage and screen in Hollywood, also director/
producer.

The Sin of the Mothers	1914
The Juggernaut	1914
The Goddess	1915
Son of Davy Crockett	1941
Lady From Louisiana	1941
Mrs. Miniver	1942
My Favorite Blonde	1942
A Yank at Eton	1942
Tish	1943
Today I Hang	1944
The Adventures of Mark Twain	1944
Kitty	1945
Down Missouri Way	1946
Pursued	1947
Magic Town	1947
The Sign of the Ram	1948
Fighting Mad	1948
The Shanghai Chest	1948
The Secret Beyond the Door	1948
Samson and Delilah	1949

DON SHARP (1922-   )

Australian-born director and stage actor who appeared in very
occasional films.

Ha'penny Breeze	1950
The Planter's Wife	1952
The Cruel Sea	1953
Appointment in London	1953
The Stolen Airliner	1955

C. MONTAGUE SHAW (1883-1968)

Australian character star of the thirties and forties in Hollywood.

The Set Up	1926
The Water Hole	1928
Behind That Curtain	1929
Morgan's Last Raid	1929
Square Shoulders	1930
The Silent Witness	1932
Pack Up Your Troubles	1932
Sherlock Holmes	1932
Cynara	1932
Letty Lynton	1932
Rasputin and the Empress	1932
Big Brain	1933
The Masquerader	1933
Today We Live	1933
Cavalcade	1933
Queen Christina	1933
Gabriel Over the White House	1933
Shock	1934
Fog	1934
Riptide	1934
Sisters Under the Skin	1934
The House of Rothschild	1934
Les Miserables	1935
A Tale of Two Cities	1935
Vanessa: Her Love Story	1935
Becky Sharp	1935
David Copperfield	1935
Two Sinners	1935
I Live for Love	1935
The Story of Louis Pasteur	1936
Undersea Kingdom	1936
The Leathernecks Have Landed	1936
My American Wife	1936
King of Burlesque	1936
Riders of the Whistling Skull	1937
The Frame Up	1937
Parole Racket	1937
The Sheik Steps Out	1937
A Nation Aflame	1937
Ready Willing and Able	1937

The King & the Chorus Girl	1937
Mars Attacks the World	1938
Four Men and a Prayer	1938
Little Miss Broadway	1938
Suez	1938
Mr. Moto's Last Warning	1939
Adventures of Sherlock Holmes	1939
The Three Musketeers	1939
The Rains Came	1939
Stanley and Livingstone	1939
My Son, My Son	1940
The Gay Caballero	1940
Charlie Chan's Murder Cruise	1940
Dick Tracy vs. Crime Inc.	1941
Hard Guy	1941
Burma Convoy	1941
Charley's Aunt	1941
Thunder Birds	1942
Random Harvest	1942
Pride of the Yankees	1942
Nazi Spy Ring	1942
G-Men vs. the Black Dragon	1943
Appointment in Berlin	1943
Faces in the Fog	1944
An Angel Comes to Brooklyn	1945
Tonight and Every Night	1945
Confidential Agent	1945
Road to the Big House	1946
Thunder in the Valley	1947

VICTORIA SHAW (1935-   )

Australian leading lady of occasional films in Hollywood.

Cattle Station	1954
The Eddy Duchin Story	1956
The Crimson Kimono	1959
I Aim at the Stars	1960
Alvarez Kelly	1966
To Trap a Spy	1966
Westworld	1973

EWEN SOLON (1917-1985)

Versatile New Zealand character player of films and television,
notable as Sergeant Lucas in TV series Maigret (1970).

London Belongs to Me	1948
Vengeance Is Mine	1949
The Naked Earth	1950
Assassin for Hire	1951
Valley of the Eagles	1951
The Rossiter Case	1951
Mystery Junction	1951
The Story of Robin Hood	1952
Crow Hollow	1952
Ghost Ship	1952
The Sword and the Rose	1953
Rob Roy the Highland Rogue	1953
The End of the Road	1954
Night Plane to Amsterdam	1955
Murder Anonymous	1955
Jumping for Joy	1955
The Dam Busters	1955
The Dark Avenger	1955
Who Done It?	1956
1984	1956
Lost	1956
Behind the Headlines	1956
Robbery Under Arms	1957
Yangtse Incident	1957
The Story of Esther Costello	1957
There's Always a Thrusday	1957
Account Rendered	1957
The Black Ice	1957
Accused	1957
English Family Robinson	1957
Murder Reported	1957
The Devil's Pass	1958
The Silent Enemy	1958
The White Trap	1959
Stranglers of Bombay	1959
Hound of the Baskervilles	1959
Jack the Ripper	1959
Tarzan the Magnificent	1960
The Sundowners	1960
Terror of the Tongs	1961

Curse of the Werewolf	1961
Mystery Submarine	1963
Infamous Conduct	1966
Dead Men Running	1970
Moving On	1972
The Message	1976
Kidnapped	1978
The Spaceman and King Arthur	1979
A Nightingale Sang in Berkeley Square	1980
The Lion of the Desert	1981
Fair Stood the Wind for France	1981
Into the Labyrinth	1982
The Nutcracker Suite	1982
The Wicked Lady	1983
Master of the Game	1984

BRUCE SPENCE

Australian actor of the 1970s and 1980s in occasional films; also on TV.

Stork	1974
Three Old Friends	1975
The Cars That Ate Paris	1975
The Firm Man	1976
The Great McCarthy	1976
Eliza Fraser	1976
Let the Balloon Go	1976
Mad Dog Morgan	1976
Oz	1977
Newsfront	1978
Dimboola	1979
Deadline	1981
Mad Max II	1982
The Return of Captain Invincible	1983
Where the Green Ants Dream	1984
Mad Max III	1985
Birdsville	1986
Bullseye	1987
Once Upon a Weekend	1987
The Year My Voice Broke	1987
Nikky and Pete	1987

JOHN STANTON

Strong Australian supporting actor who has made a few impressive films.

Dusty	1983
Kitty and the Bagman	1983
Phar Lap	1983
Tai-Pan	1986
Great Expectations	1987

MINNIE STEELE (1881-1949)

Australian actress in Hollywood with vaudeville experience. Occasional, sporadic films.

Christie	1924
Baby Peggy	1924
The Darling of New York	1926
A Feather in Her Hat	1935
The Wife Takes a Flyer	1942

PAMELA STEPHENSON (1951-)

Lovely New Zealand leading lady of films and television; TV series: Not the Nine O'Clock News.

Stand Up Virgin Soldiers	1977
The Comeback	1978
Funny Man	1979
Man from the South	1980
History of the World Part I	1981
The Secret Policeman's Other Ball	1982
Superman III	1983
Scandalous	1983
Bloodbath at the House of Death	1983
Finders Keepers	1984
Lost Empires	1986
Les Patterson Saves the World	1987
Those Dear Departed	1987

BETTY STOCKFELD (1905-1966)

Australian character actress of stage (since 1924) and films,
popular during the thirties.

What Price Glory	1926
Captivation	1931
City of Song	1931
77 Park Lane	1931
Money for Nothing	1932
Life Goes On	1932
The Impassive Footman	1932
Maid of the Mountains	1932
King of the Ritz	1932
Women in Chains	1932
Farewell to Love	1933
Lord of the Manor	1933
Anne One Hundred	1933
The Man Who Changed His Name	1934
The Battle	1934
Brides to Be	1934
The Lad	1935
Runaway Ladies	1935
Under Proof	1936
Beloved Vagabond	1936
Dishonour Bright	1936
Who's Your Lady Friend?	1937
Club de Femmes	1937
I See Ice	1938
The Slipper Episode	1938
Nine Bachelors	1941
Hard Steel	1942
Flying Fortress	1942
Derriere la Facade	1942
Edward and Caroline	1950
The Girl Who Couldn't Quite	1950
The Lovers of Lisbon	1955
Guilty	1956
True as a Turtle	1957
Forbidden Desire	1958

PETER SUMNER

Australian stage and television performer who has also made
several motion pictures.

Color Me Dead	1969
Ned Kelly	1970
The Chant of Jimmie Blacksmith	1980
The Survivor	1981
The Dismissal	1983
Bush Christmas	1984
Army Wives	1987

COLIN TAPLEY (1911-   )

Sturdy New Zealand Character actor of stage and screen, often in cameo roles. Also in Hollywood.

Come On Marines	1934
Double Door	1934
Search for Beauty	1934
Murder at the Vantities	1934
The Pursuit of Happiness	1934
The Black Room	1935
Lives of a Bengal Lancer	1935
Becky Sharp	1935
The Last Outpost	1935
Peter Ibbotsen	1935
The Crusades	1935
Early to Bed	1936
The Return of Sophie Lang	1936
Till We Meet Again	1936
The Sky Parade	1936
Thank You Jeeves	1936
Marriage	1936
The Preview Murder Mystery	1936
The Crime Nobody Saw	1937
King of Gamblers	1937
A Night of Mystery	1937
Bulldog Drummond Escapes	1937
Wild Money	1938
Booloo	1938
If I Were King	1938
Storm Over Bengal	1938
The Light That Failed	1939
Women in War	1940
Arizona	1941
Samson and Delilah	1949
Cloudburst	1950
Wings of Danger	1951

Angels One Five	1952
Wide Boy	1952
Strange Stories	1953
Three Steps to the Gallows	1953
The Steel Key	1953
Noose for a Lady	1953
White Fire	1954
The Diamond	1954
Late Night Final	1954
The Dam Busters	1955
Little Red Monkey	1955
Barbados Quest	1955
Stranglehold	1955
Stranger in Town	1957
Blood of the Vampire	1958
The Safecracker	1958
Innocent Meeting	1959
Man Accused	1959
High Jump	1959
Night Train for Inverness	1960
An Honourable Murder	1960
Compelled	1960
So Evil So Young	1961
The Lamp in Assassin Mews	1962
Emergency	1962
Strongroom	1962
Gang War	1962
Paranoiac	1963
Shadow of Fear	1963
Fraulein Doktor	1968

JOHN TATE (1914-1979)

Australian actor seen on TV and in a few motion pictures.

Smiley Gets a Gun	1958
On the Beach	1959
It's All Happening	1963
Invasion	1966
Black Peter	1968
Bindle	1968
Julius Caesar	1970

ROD TAYLOR (1929-)

Australian leading man of stage and screen, primarily in Hollywood from 1955; often seen as tough hero. TV series: <u>Hong</u>
<u>Kong</u> (1960); <u>Bearcats</u> (1971); <u>The Oregon Trail</u> (1976); <u>Outlaws</u>
(1987).

The Stewart Expedition	1951
King of the Coral Sea	1954
Long John Silver	1955
The Virgin Queen	1955
The Browning Version	1955
Killer Whale	1955
The Last Day on Earth	1955
Top Gun	1955
The Rack	1956
World Without End	1956
Hell on Frisco Bay	1956
The Catered Affair	1956
Giant	1956
Raintree County	1957
The Young Years	1957
Step Down to Terror	1958
Verdict of Three	1958
The Great Gatsby	1958
Best House in the Valley	1958
The Long March	1958
The Raider	1958
Separate Tables	1958
Ask Any Girl	1959
Misalliance	1959
The Story of Marjorie Reardon	1959
And When the Sky Was Opened	1959
Capital Gains	1960
Early to Die	1960
Thunder in the Night	1960
Queen of the Amazons	1960
The Time Machine	1960
101 Dalmatians (voice)	1961
The Ordeal of Dr. Shannon	1962
Seven Seas to Calais	1963
The Birds	1963
The VIPs	1963
A Gathering of Eagles	1963
Sunday in New York	1964

Fate Is the Hunter	1964
36 Hours	1965
Young Cassisy	1965
Do Not Disturb	1965
The Liquidator	1966
The Glass Bottom Boat	1966
The Mercenaries	1967
Hotel	1967
Chuka	1967
Hell Is for Heroes	1968
Nobody Runs Forever	1968
Zabriskie Point	1970
The Man Who Had Power Over Women	1970
Darker Than Amber	1970
Powderkeg	1971
The Train Robbers	1972
Family Flight	1972
Trader Horn	1973
The Deadly Trackers	1973
Hell River	1974
Partizan	1974
The Heroes	1975
Blondy	1975
A Matter of Wife & Death	1975
The Oregon Trail	1976
The Picture Show Man	1977
An Eye for an Eye	1978
Jamaican Gold	1979
Six Graves for Rogan	1980
Cry of the Innocent	1980
The Hitchhiker	1980
Jacqueline Bouvier Kennedy	1981
Hellinger's Law	1981
Charles & Diana: A Royal Love Story	1982
On the Run	1983
Masquerade	1983
Marbella	1985
The Face	1985
Half Nelson	1985
Mask of Murder	1985
Outlaws	1986

DESMOND TESTER (1919-)

Juvenile player of the thirties, latterly in Australia.

Late Extra	1935
Midshipman Easy	1935
Tudor Rose	1936
Sabotage	1936
A Woman Alone	1936
Beloved Vagabond	1936
Non Stop New York	1937
The Drum	1938
The Stars Look Down	1939
An Englishman's Home	1939
The Turners of Prospect Road	1947
Barry Mackenzie Holds His Own	1974
Save the Lady	1981
The Wild Duck	1983
The Explorers	1984
Brothers	1984

JACK THOMPSON (1940-)

Strong, dependable Australian leading man of the 1970s and 1980s. Also TV.

Outback	1971
Wake in Fright	1971
No Roses for Michael	1972
Jock Petersen	1975
The Taking of Christina	1976
Mad Dog Morgan	1976
Scobie Malone	1977
The Journalist	1978
Because He's My Friend	1978
Caddie	1979
The Chant of Jimmie Blacksmith	1980
The Club	1980
Breaker Morant	1980
The Earthling	1980
Bad Blood	1981
Sunday Too Far Away	1981
The Letter	1982
A Woman Called Golda	1982
The Man from Snowy River	1982

Merry Christmas, Mr. Lawrence	1983
Waterfront	1983
Tai Chi	1984
Flesh and Blood	1984
Sea Trial	1985
Burke and Wills	1985
Joe Wilson	1986
Ground Zero	1986
The Last Frontier	1986
The Man from Snowy River II	1987
Kojak: The Investigation	1987

SIGRID THORNTON

Youthful Australian leading lady of the 1970s and 1980s, also much on television.

Matlock	1974
Division 4	1974
Homicide	1975
Young Ramsay	1976
Cop Shop	1976
Skyways	1976
Bellbird	1977
Case for the Defence	1977
Chopper Squad	1977
The Young Doctors	1977
The Prisoner	1978
The FJ Holden	1978
The Sullivans	1979
Certain Women	1979
The Getting of Wisdom	1979
Truckies	1980
Lawson's Mates	1980
Outbreak of Love	1980
Waterloo Street	1981
Hotel Story	1981
Partners	1981
The Man from Snowy River	1982
All the Rivers Run	1983
1915	1984
The Boy in the Bush	1985
Street Hero	1986
The Far Country	1986

Slate, Wyn, and Me	1987
Great Expectations	1987
The Man from Snowy River II	1987
The Lighthorsemen	1987

FRANK THRING

Australian character and supporting performer of occasional films and TV; also in Hollywood. TV series: Skippy the Bush Kangaroo (1969) (as Dr. Alexander Stark).

A Question of Adultery	1958
The Vikings	1958
Ben Hur	1959
King of Kings	1961
El Cid	1961
Age of Consent	1969
Ned Kelly	1970
Alvin Rides Again	1974
The Man from Hong Kong	1975
Mad Dog Morgan	1976
Mad Max III	1985
Bullamakanka	1985
The Marsupials	1987

CHARLES TINGWELL (1917-)

Australian character actor of television and screen, often seen as characters of humility. TV series: Homicide (1974-75).

Always Another Dawn	1948
Bitter Springs	1950
Kangaroo	1952
The Desert Rats	1953
Captain Thunderbolt	1953
King of the Coral Sea	1954
Smiley	1956
The Shiralee	1957
Life in Emergency Ward Ten	1958
Bobbikins	1959
Cone of Silence	1960
Tarzan the Magnificent	1960
Murder She Said	1962

Murder at the Gallop	1963
Murder Ahoy!	1964
Beware of the Dog	1964
Murder Most Foul	1965
The Secret of Blood Island	1965
Thunderbirds Are Go	1966
Dracula Prince of Darkness	1966
Nobody Runs Forever	1968
The Solitary Cyclist	1968
Jock Petersen	1975
Eliza Fraser	1976
Is There Anybody There?	1976
End Play	1976
Summerfield	1977
Money Movers	1978
Breaker Morant	1980
Freedom	1982
Annie's Coming Cout	1983
All the Rivers Run	1983
Puberty Blues	1984
My First Wife	1984
Gone to Ground	1985
Handle with Care	1986
Windrider	1986

TOKE TOWNLEY (1912-1984)

Australian character and supporting actor who was popular during the fifties, also on TV in series Emmerdale Farm (as Sam Pearson).

Lady Godiva Rides Again	1951
Treasure Hunt	1952
Cosh Boy	1952
Meet Me Tonight	1952
The Broken Horseshoe	1953
Meet Mr. Lucifer	1953
Innocents in Paris	1953
Time Gentlemen Please	1953
Fast and Loose	1954
Bang You're Dead	1954
The Runaway Bus	1954
The Men of Sherwood Forest	1954
The Quatermass Experiment	1955

Doctor at Sea	1955
John and Julie	1955
Now and Forever	1956
Three Men in a Boat	1956
The Admirable Crichton	1957
Carry On Admiral	1957
Barnacle Bill	1957
A Cry from the Streets	1958
Law and Disorder	1958
Look Back in Anger	1959
Libel	1959
The Missing Note	1961
HMS Defiant	1962
Doctor in Distress	1963
The Chalk Garden	1964
The Legend of Young Dick Turpin	1965
The Red-Headed League	1966
Scars of Dracula	1970
Clouds of Witness	1973
Chimpmates	1977

NOEL TREVARTHEN

Supporting performer of films who is also a frequent TV player; also latterly in Australia.

Your Money or Your Wife	1959
Escort for Hire	1960
Backfire	1962
Fate Takes a Hand	1962
To Have and to Hold	1963
Material Witness	1965
It	1966
The Vengeance of Fu Manchu	1967
Corruption	1968
Take Me High	1973
The Abdication	1974
Great Expectations	1975
All I Want Is You	1976
Dusty	1983
The Facts of Life Down Under	1987
The High Country	1987
To Market, to Market	1987
Anzacs	1987

MARTIN VAUGHAN

Splendid Australian supporting actor of occasional films and
television.

Between Wars	1974
Picnic at Hanging Rock	1976
Ride a Wild Pony	1976
Just Out of Reach	1979
Alison's Birthday	1980
We of the Never Never	1982
Phar Lap	1983
The Dismissal	1984
Constance	1987
Great Expectations	1987

MAVIS VILLIERS

Australian supporting actress of stage and screen who began
her career as a juvenile performer in Hollywood.

Little Lord Fauntleroy	1922
A Lady's Morals	1930
King of the Castle	1936
Double Alibi	1937
In Your Garden	1938
An Englishman's Home	1939
The Nursemaid Who Disappeared	1939
Saloon Bar	1940
Sailors Don't Care	1940
Gasbags	1940
Hi Gang	1941
South American George	1941
One Exciting Night	1944
Take My Life	1947
Corridor of Mirrors	1948
Pool of London	1951
Too Many Detectives	1953
Time Is My Enemy	1954
The Mouse That Roared	1959
A Touch of Larceny	1959
Suddenly Last Summer	1960
Victim	1961
The Roman Spring of Mrs. Stone	1962

The Boys	1962
The Haunting	1963
Promise Her Anything	1966
Laughter in the Dark	1969
Straight On Till Morning	1972
Baxter	1973
No Sex Please We're British	1973
Cat and Mouse	1974

MARGARET VYNER (1915-)

Lovely Australian leading lady and second lead of stage and films; married to Hugh Williams; mother of Simon Williams.

The Flying Doctor	1936
Sensation	1937
Cavalier of the Streets	1937
Midnight Menace	1937
Incident in Shanghai	1938
Sailing Along	1938
Climbing High	1938
Dangerous Comment	1940
The Patient Vanishes	1941
The Young Mr. Pitt	1942
The Lamp Still Burns	1943
Give Me the Stars	1944
Twilight Hour	1944
Mr. Emmanuel	1944
Encore	1951
Something Money Can't Buy	1952

RACHEL WARD (1957-)

Australian leading lady of the eighties, also in Hollywood. Married to Bryan Brown.

Night School	1981
Three Blind Mice	1981
Sharkey's Machine	1981
Dead Men Don't Wear Plaid	1982
The Thorn Birds	1982
Out of the Past	1983
Against All Odds	1983

Running Man	1983
The Final Terror	1984
Fortress	1985
The Umbrella Woman	1986
Hotel Colonial	1986
The Good Wife	1986
The Legendary Life of Ernest Heming- way	1987
Ring of Scorpio	1987

JOHN WARWICK (1905-1972)

Australian character actor and former leading man who was seen
frequently as crook and policeman alike.

In the Wake of the Bounty	1933
The Squatter's Daughter	1933
The Silence of Dean Maitland	1934
Down on the Farm	1935
Find the Lady	1936
Orphan of the Wilderness	1936
Lucky Jade	1937
Double Alibi	1937
Catch as Catch Can	1937
When the Poppies Bloom Again	1937
Passenger to London	1937
Ticket of Leave Man	1937
Riding High	1937
Bad Boy	1938
A Yank at Oxford	1938
John Halifax, Gentleman	1938
This Man Is News	1938
21 Days	1938
Me and My Pal	1939
Dead Men Are Dangerous	1939
The Mind of Mr. Reeder	1939
The Face at the Window	1939
The Flying Fifty-Five	1939
All at Sea	1939
Case of the Frightened Lady	1940
Spare a Copper	1940
The Saint's Vacation	1941
Danny Boy	1941
My Wife's Family	1941
The Missing Million	1942

The Day Will Dawn	1942
Talk About Jacqueline	1942
Woman to Woman	1946
Dancing with Crime	1947
Teheran	1947
While I Live	1947
The Franchise Affair	1951
The Lavender Hill Mob	1951
Never Look Back	1952
Circumstantial Evidence	1952
Escape Route	1953
Trouble in Store	1953
Street Corner	1953
Parlour Trick	1953
The Accused	1953
The Red Dress	1954
Bang You're Dead	1954
Up to His Neck	1954
Dangerous Voyage	1954
One Just Man	1955
Contraband Spain	1955
The Mysterious Bullet	1955
The Long Arm	1956
The Tyburn Case	1957
Just My Luck	1957
Gideon's Day	1958
Print of Death	1958
The Crossroad Gallows	1958
Law and Disorder	1958
The Square Peg	1958
Horrors of the Black Museum	1959
The Desperate Man	1959
Murder at Site Three	1959
The Fourth Square	1961
Go to Blazes	1962
Adam's Woman	1970

JOHN WATERS

Versatile Australian leading actor and sometimes supporting
player in films and TV.

Angel Gear	1976
End Play	1976

Eliza Fraser	1976
Summerfield	1977
Weekend of Shadows	1978
Cass	1979
The Getting of Wisdom	1980
Breaker Morant	1980
The Z Men	1981
Multiple Maniac	1982
All the Rivers Run	1983
High Country	1984
Act II	1984
Demolition	1984
The Scalp Merchant	1985
The Perfectionist	1985
Passion Flower	1985
I Can't Get Started	1985
Going Sane	1986
Alice to Nowhere	1986
Something Wild	1986
Nancy Wake	1987
Boulevard of Broken Dreams	1987
Bodily Harm	1987
The Breaker	1987

ALBERT WHELAN (1875-1961)

Australian supporting and character actor of the 1930s and 1940s, also a popular variety artist. Former accountant and engineer.

An Intimate Interlude	1928
The Man from Chicago	1930
O.K. Chief	1930
Matinee Idol	1933
Anything Might Happen	1934
Dance Band	1935
Stars on Parade	1936
Educated Evans	1936
The Girl in the Taxi	1937
Action For Slander	1937
The Green Cockatoo	1937
Mad About Money	1937
Thank Evans	1938
Kate Plus Ten	1938
Danny Boy	1941

Candlelight in Algeria	1943
English Without Tears	1944
Keep It Clean	1956

FRANK WILSON

Australian supporting player of stage, occasional films, and TV.

Patrick	1978
Money Movers	1978
The Journalist	1979
Breaker Morant	1980

JOAN WINFIELD (1919-1978)

Australian actress of the forties and fifties in Hollywood.

Bullets for O'Hara	1941
The Gorilla Man	1942
Mission to Moscow	1943
Murder on the Waterfront	1943
Adventures of Mark Twain	1944
Stolen Life	1946
The Imerfect Lady	1947
Johnny Belinda	1948
Queen for a Day	1951
The Egyptian	1954

JOHN WOOD

Australian supporting and character player of stage and screen; former commercial artist and banana farmer.

The Girl in the Crowd	1934
The Last Days of Pompeii	1935
Full Circle	1935
The Case of Gabriel Perry	1935
To Catch a Thief	1936
Over She Goes	1937
Housemaster	1938
Hold My Hand	1938
Oh Boy!	1938
Luck of the Navy	1938

Black Eyes	1939
An Englishman's Home	1939
Stolen Face	1952
Idol on Parade	1958
Two-Way Stretch	1960
Let's Get Married	1960
The Challenge	1960
Invasion Quartet	1961
The Rebel	1961
Postman's Knock	1962
Live Now Pay Later	1962
That Kind of Girl	1963
Just for Fun	1963
Mouse on the Moon	1963
Just Like a Woman	1966
One More Time	1970
Which Way to the Front?	1970
The Office Picnic	1973

CONSTANCE WORTH (1915-1963)

Australian actress in Hollywood who began as a child performer;
also sometimes on stage.

Heart and Soul	1919
The Starting Point	1919
The Non-Conformist Parson	1919
Wisp O' the Woods	1919
Fate's Plaything	1920
The Education of Nicky	1921
Bachelor's Baby	1922
No. 7 Brick Row	1922
Within the Maze	1923
Love in the Welsh Hills	1924
China Passage	1937
The Windjammer	1937
Mystery of the White Room	1939
Angels Over Broadway	1940
Meet Boston Blackie	1941
Borrowed Hero	1941
Suspicion	1941
When Johnny Comes Marching Home	1942
Boston Blackie Goes Hollywood	1942
City Without Men	1943

Crime Doctor	1943
G-Men vs. the Black Dragon	1943
Crime Doctor's Strangest Case	1943
Cyclone Prairie Rangers	1944
Sagebrush Heroes	1944
Why Girls Leave Home	1945
Kid Sister	1945
Dillinger	1945
Deadline at Dawn	1946
Sensation Hunters	1946
Western Renegades	1949
The Set-Up	1950

BIBLIOGRAPHY

Adamson, Judith. Australian Film Posters 1906-60. Sydney:
Currency Press, 1978.

Baxter, John. The Australian Cinema. Sydney: Angus &
Robertson, 1970.

Bertrand, Ina. Film Censorship in Australia. Queensland:
Queensland Press, 1978.

Carroll, Brian. The Menzies Years. Sydney: Cassell Press,
1977.

Dundy, Elaine. Finch, Bloody Finch. New York: Holt,
Rinehart & Winston, 1980.

Faulkner, Trader. Peter Finch: A Biography. London:
Angus & Robertson, 1979.

Hall, Ken G. Australian Film, the Inside Story. Sydney:
Summit Books, 1980.

Hall, Ken G. Directed By Ken G. Hall. Melbourne: Lansdowne
Press, 1977.

Horne, Donald. The Australian People. Sydney: Angus &
Robertson, 1972.

Monkman, Noel. The Quest of the Curly-Tailed Horses. Sydney:
Angus & Robertson, 1964.

Pike, Andrew, and Ross Cooper. Australian Film 1900-1977.
London: Oxford University Press, 1980 .

Porter, Hal. Stars of the Australian Stage and Screen.
Sydney: Halstead Press, 1965.

Reade, Eric. The Australian Screen. Melbourne: Lansdowne
Press, 1975.

Reade, Eric. Australian Silent Films. Melbourne: Lansdowne
Press, 1970.

Reade, Eric. History & Heartburn: The Saga of Australian
Films 1896-1978. Sydney: Harper and Row, 1979.

Rees, Leslie. The Making of Australian Drama. Sydney:
Angus & Robertson, 1973.

Ritchie, John. Australia as Once We Were. Melbourne: Heine-
mann Press, 1975.

Shirley, Graham, and Brian Adams. Australian Cinema: The
First 80 Years. Sydney: Angus & Robertson and Currency Press, 1983.

Souter, Gavin. The Lion & the Kangaroo. Sydney: Collins
Press, 1978.

Stratton, David. The Last New Wave. Sydney & Melbourne:
Angus & Robertson, 1980.

Thoms, Albie. Polemics For a New Cinema. Sydney: Wild &
Woolley, 1978.

Thorne, Ross. Picture Palace Architecture in Australia.
Melbourne: Sun Books, 1976.

Thornhill, Michael. The Australian Film. Sydney: Current
Affairs, 1966.

Wasson, Mervyn. The Beginnings of Australian Cinema.
Melbourne: AFI Press, 1964.

White, David. Australian Movies to the World. Sydney:
Fontana Australia; Melbourne: Cinema Papers, 1984.